181513

Lat

Welcome to the Mansion

An Introductory Guide to the Study of Rhetoric

John Harrigan, PhD

Copley Custom Textbooks
An imprint of XanEdu Custom Publishing

Copyright © 2007 by John Harrigan. All rights reserved
Printed in the United States of America

ISBN-13: 978-1-58152-542-7
ISBN-10: 1-58152-542-7

No part of this book may be reproduced in any manner without written permission from the publisher.

Acknowledgments:

pp. 10–23: From *The Rhetorical Tradition* by Patricia Bizzell and Bruce Herzberg. Copyright © 1990 by Bedford/St. Martin's. Reproduced by permission of Bedford/St. Martin's.

pp. 34–56: From *On Rhetoric: A Theory of Civic Discourse*, edited by George A. Kennedy. Copyright © 2007 by Oxford University Press, NY. Reprinted by permission of the publisher via the Copyright Clearance Center.

pp. 66–74, 77–80, 166–170: From *Rhetorical Theory, An Introduction* (with InfoTrac(R)), first edition, by Timothy Borchers. Copyright © 2006. Reprinted with permission of Wadsworth, a division of Thomson Learning: www.thomsonrights.com. Fax 800-730-2215.

pp. 76, 144–164: From *Rhetoric and Human Consciousness* by Craig R. Smith. Copyright © 2003 by Waveland Press, Inc., Long Grove, IL. Reprinted by permission of Waveland Press, Inc.

pp. 82–115: From *The Rhetoric of Western Thought* by James Golden. Copyright © 2003. Published by Kendall/Hunt Publishing Company.

pp. 118–133: From *The History and Theory of Rhetoric: An Introduction* by James Herrick. Published by Allyn & Bacon, Boston, MA. Copyright © 2005 by Pearson Education. Reprinted by permission of the publisher.

pp. 136–141: From *Introducing Philosophy: A Text with Integrated Readings*, fourth edition, by Robert Solomon. Copyright © 1988. Reprinted with permission of Wadsworth, a division of Thomson Learning: www.thomsonrights.com. Fax 800-730-2215.

pp. 172–179: As appeared in *The Humanistic Psychologist,* Vol. 18, No. 1, 1990. Copyright © 1990 by Lawrence Erlbaum Associates.

Copley Custom Textbooks
An imprint of XanEdu Custom Publishing
138 Great Road
Acton, MA 01720
800-562-2147

Contents

Section One: Welcome to the Mansion of Rhetoric: An Introductory Guide to the Study of Rhetoric

SECTION ONE

Welcome to the Mansion of Rhetoric: An Introductory Guide to the Study of Rhetoric

. . . to enlighten the understanding, to please the imagination, to move the passions and to influence the will.—George Campbell

I was feeling part of the scenery; I walked right out of the machinery,
My heart going boom, boom, boom;
"Hey," he said "Grab your things; I've come to take you home."—Peter Gabriel

Welcome to the Mansion of Rhetoric, home to the extraordinary influence of language and thought. It is here that the capacity of human communication is studied, practiced and realized. The Mansion is an expansive architectural wonder. The foundations were built centuries ago and new additions are still being constructed to this day. There are many interconnecting hallways and stairwells that lead to a variety of rooms that differ in size, style and function. I'm sure you'll find, as we explore this engaging environment, that the attributes of rhetoric are sometimes practical and sometimes mysterious, but always pertinent to influential forms of communication. Within these walls and upon the grounds surrounding the Mansion dwells the profound utility of expression. It is with thoughtfulness and enthusiasm that we will tour the Mansion of Rhetoric and it is here that I hope you make yourself at home.

Rhetoric is the relation between thought and expression.—William Covino

I was just guessing, at numbers and figures, pulling your puzzles apart.
Questions of science, science and progress,

Do not speak as loud as my heart.—Coldplay

Rhetoric is a vast and diverse subject with a variety of defining characteristics. Fundamentally, rhetoric can be understood as the art of effective and persuasive use of communication. It is from this basic definition that we will expand the meaning of rhetoric which encompasses a confluence of interdisciplinary studies including: linguistics, philosophy, sociology, semantics, mass media and psychology. We will see that rhetoric has an edge to it in political and legal proceedings. We will come to understand the rhetorical devices in arts of poetry and storytelling. We will encounter epistemological theories that are united with rhetorical trends. We will realize the significance of the ethics behind rhetoric; with the power of language comes a responsibility of how that power is directed. However, as we move from room to room in the Mansion of Rhetoric we will be reminded that at the heart of rhetoric is a form of expression conceived from a desire to be understood.

Rhetoric is the faculty of discovering all the available means of persuasion in any situation.—Aristotle

Biggy, Biggy, Biggy can't you see,
Sometimes your words just hypnotize me.—Notorious BIG

Upon entering the Mansion of Rhetoric we will find ourselves in the Grand Foyer of Greek Rhetorical Theory. It is here that we will focus our studies on Aristotle and his systematic and scientific approach which has been the foundation for studies in rhetoric. We will start with the three appeals or proofs as they are called. The first is rational appeal. This proof utilizes logic as a mode of persuasion. The second is emotional appeal. This proof deals with feelings and passions in convincing forms. The third is ethical appeal. This proof underscores the vital importance of appealing to one's sense of values while ascertaining the speaker's integrity.

The Forms of Discourse or Speaking Occasions will also be noticed. The first occasion is Forensic Discourse which is judicial in nature and justice hopefully being the outcome. The second occasion is Deliberative Discourse which is political in nature taking into consideration community and national issues. The third occasion is Epideictic Discourse which fundamentally is ceremonial and demonstrative in principle usually dealing with elements of praise or blame.

We will also encounter Isocrates, another Greek philosopher known as an educator within the discipline of speech. We will discuss his Three Essentials of Learning: Natural Ability, Training and Practice. He will also serve as a bridge to the Roman Rhetoricians who continued his notion creating the citizen-orator.

This is one of the largest areas in the Mansion of Rhetoric. We will continue to regard the basis of Greek Rhetoric as we move forward in our tour.

I shall be telling this with a sigh, somewhere ages and ages hence:
Two roads diverged in a wood, and I,
I took the one less traveled by,
And that had made all the difference.—Robert Frost

Come to send, not condescend.
Transcendental consequence is to transcend
where we are and who we are.—Pearl Jam

The next areas we encounter in the Mansion of Rhetoric are the Roman Rhetoricians, Cicero and Quintilian being the philosophers of focus. As influenced by Isocrates, the Romans were interested in developing students of rhetoric into Philosophers, Orators and Statesmen. Their approach was to require a broad liberal arts education in addition to having students develop a deep sense of character.

The Romans also furthered the organization of rhetoric with the Five Cannons of Classical Rhetoric. The first canon is invention, dealing with the creation and development of the initial message in a rhetorical expression. The second canon is dispositio which discusses the various methods of organizing the message. The third canon is elocutio. This canon explains the different styles of language use. The fourth canon is memoria which corresponds directly to the faculty of memory and the speaker's ability to recall. The fifth canon is pronunciatio. This area reveals notions of voice control, gesturing and appearance is it applies to numerous rhetorical situations.

The great foundation of figurative language
rests on the association of ideas.—John Adams

Hope is the thing with feathers, that perches in the soul,
And sings the tune without words,
And never stops at all.—Emily Dickinson

We will then move to abundant gardens that surround the Mansion of Rhetoric. It is here that we will find meaningful figures of speech and other uses of language that depart from customary construction, order, use and significance. We will encounter the poetic nature of language studying the trope and other rhetoric devices that use words in other than their literal sense. As gardens have different types of flowers, there are different kinds of tropes. Our main focus will be on the function of the metaphor, but we will also see the simile, hyperbole, personification, metonymy and allegory, to name a few.

To quote John Adams again, "Gather fragrance from the whole paradise of science and learn to distill from your lips the honey of persuasion." It is my hope that the metaphors gathered in the gardens will have a lasting impact on your study of rhetoric.

The goal of genius, thus the goal of rhetoric is not to persuade the
audience but to transport them out of themselves.—Longinus

If I could, through myself, set your spirit free
I'd lead your heart away
See you break, break away
Into the light and to the day.—U2

As we venture back through the hallways, we will next meet the Belletristic Movement. This area serves to bridge the classical section of our studies with post-renaissance developments in rhetoric. The Belletristic Movement was an eclectic philosophy combining poetry, history, arts and education. It continued to evaluate rhetoric as an art form through the following areas: taste and artistic quality, criticism and the evaluative process, genius and the identification of intelligence, perspicuity and the importance of clarity, precision and the accuracy of thought and lastly beauty and all its aesthetic considerations.

Another evaluative concept the Belletristic Movement analyzed was the sublime. We will cover Longinus and his work, "On The Sublime" and also look at other philosophers' interpretations of sublimity. It is here that rhetoric transcends the confines of mere eloquence and becomes the principal mode of reflective philosophy.

Knowledge is power.—Francis Bacon

If you knew all the answers and could give it to the masses,
Would you do it?
With all of that power,
What would you do?—Flaming Lips

One of the largest areas in the Mansion of Rhetoric is the wing housing Epistemology. It is here that we will seek a philosophy of knowledge. It is here that we will consider the nature and limits of human knowledge, challenging conventional forms of logic and eventually calling into question our knowledge of reality. Fundamentally, though, we will attempt to explain two key questions: What is knowledge and how is it communicated?

After a brief introduction of empiricism via Francis Bacon and John Locke, we will turn our attention to René Descartes and his ideas on rationalism. We will move on to Giambattista Vico and the foundations of social science where rhetoric is the poetic expression of knowledge thus transforming society. As we further explore this area we will find epistemological trends progressing toward psychology and the faculties of the mind. David Hume and George Campbell will show us a continually evolving concept of rhetoric through their discussion of the four faculties of the mind: the understanding, the imagination, the passions and the will. All of these faculties must be stimulated if true rhetorical communication is to be achieved.

What lies behind us and what lies before us are tiny matters compared to what lies within us.—Ralph Waldo Emerson

Imagine no possessions, I wonder if you can
No need for greed or hunger,

A brotherhood of man
Imagine all the people, sharing all the world.—John Lennon

Moving through the Mansion of Rhetoric will encounter one of the most vital aspects of our study: ethics. The ethical dimensions of rhetoric are numerous. "How" something is said is just as important as "what" is said. This notion emphasizes the principle that the communicator had the freedom to determine the structure of the message; choice is inherent to the utility of rhetoric. Furthermore, your values are disclosed in your rhetorical behavior. That is to say, "how" you communicate reveals your character.

We will look at Richard Weaver's axiological ideals and how rhetoric is the driving force in the transmission of human values.

There are no facts, only interpretations.—Friedrich Nietzsche

Oh, life is bigger,
It's bigger than you and you are not me,
The lengths that I will go to,
The distance in your eyes,
Oh no, I've said too much,
I'm losing my religion.—REM

As we round out our tour of the Mansion of Rhetoric we proceed through a collection of rooms dealing with contemporary theories in rhetoric. The first room will deal with Existentialism. Here we will meet such philosophers as Soren Kierkegaard, Friedrich Nietzsche and Jean-Paul Sartre. We will discuss the significance of the individual in a seemingly irrational world, where rhetoric allows us to express our individuality.

We will move on to semantics and the study of meaning with I. A. Richards, where once again, we will find metaphor the key to understanding. We will continue to Postmodernism and contemporary philosophers such as Michael Foucault and Jean-Francois Lyotard. We will see postmodernism as favoring multiplicity and plurality while rejecting conformist and hierarchical rationalism. This will lead to recognizing rhetoric's place with relevance to power and language.

Rhetoric should be identified with the energy inherent in effective communication.—George Kennedy

All that is now, All that is gone,
All that's to come,
And everything under the sun is in tune,
But the sun is eclipsed by the moon.—Pink Floyd

Remember that this is only the introductory tour of the Mansion of Rhetoric. We have covered a considerable amount of material that will aid in your understanding of rhetoric and its ancillary topics. There are still many rooms to see and many ideas to encounter. But through this experience it is my hope that you will have developed a certain comfort level with rhetoric, so much so that where it resides, you, as well, will feel at home.

Section Two:
A General Overview of Rhetoric

Section Two: A General Overview of Rhetoric

General Introduction

Patricia Bizzell

In parturition begins the centrality of the nervous system. The different nervous systems, through language and the ways of production, erect various communities of interests and insights, social communities varying in nature and scope. And out of the division and the community arises the "universal" rhetorical situation. — Kenneth Burke

Rhetoric has a number of overlapping meanings: the practice of oratory; the study of the strategies of effective oratory; the use of language, written or spoken, to inform or persuade; the study of the persuasive effects of language; the study of the relation between language and knowledge; the classification and use of tropes and figures; and, of course, the use of empty promises and half-truths as a form of propaganda. Nor does this list exhaust the definitions that might be given. Rhetoric is a complex discipline with a long history: It is less helpful to try to define it once and for all than to look at the many definitions it has accumulated over the years and to attempt to understand how each arose and how each still inhabits and shapes the field.

This general introduction offers an overview of the historical development of rhetoric divided into conventional chronological periods: the Classical (from the birth of rhetoric in ancient Greece to about 400 C.E.), the Medieval (to about 1400), the Renaissance (to the early seventeenth century), the Enlightenment (from the seventeenth to the end of the nineteenth century, a bit longer than in conventional usage), and the Twentieth Century. The introductions to each of the corresponding five parts of *The Rhetorical Tradition* provide a more detailed historical and theoretical picture of the development of rhetoric.

THE ORIGINS OF RHETORIC

Rhetoric in its various incarnations has been a powerful force in public affairs and in education for most of its existence since the fifth century B.C.E., when it developed in Greek probate courts and flourished under Greek democracy. Rhetoric was, first and foremost, the art of persuasive speaking. In civil disputes, persuasion established claims where no clear truth was available. Persuasive speech, too, could depose or empower tyrants, determine public policy, and administer laws. Public speaking was inseparable from the business of government and civil affairs, and early on some enterprising orators turned to teaching the art of persuasive speech as well as practicing it. Speeches required arguments that would convince and stories that would move. Speeches could be divided into parts, the parts had strategies, the strategies varied with the occasion and the audience, and the finished speech had to be memorized and finally delivered. *Rhetoric* thus came to designate both the practice of persuasive oratory and the description of ways to construct a successful speech — a complex art of great power.

Rhetoric selects, from the vast realm of human discourse, occasions for speaking and writing that can be regarded as persuasive in intent. Rhetoric categorizes the types of discourse it has selected, analyzes each of those types in terms of structure and purpose, and identifies the means for successfully constructing each type. In pursuing these goals, rhetoric comes to endorse codes for linguistic correctness and to make taxonomies of artful ways to use language. It suggests resources for evidence and argument and gives rules for accurate reasoning. And it divides the mind into faculties to which persuasive appeals, both logical and psychological, can be addressed.

The study of rhetoric dominated formal education in most of Europe and the United States until well into the nineteenth century. To study rhetoric was, for much of its history, to study Greek and Latin grammar, classical literature and history, and logic, as well as to practice the composition and delivery of speeches. But by and large, rhetoric has not been a form of inquiry, seeking to extend its scope by looking into the various uses of discourse that might be considered persuasive. Rather, it has been chiefly prescriptive, intended to teach a practical art and to provide guidelines for discourse in several well-defined social, political, and artistic arenas. Nonetheless, a vital art inevitably produces a body of theory — some of it implicit in its practical systems, some of it abstract and speculative — that investigates not only techniques and effects but philosophical underpinnings. So it is with rhetorical theory, which seeks to penetrate the complexities of communication and persuasion.

At its very inception, the study of rhetoric generated not only an elaborate system for investigating language practices but also a set of far-reaching, theoretical questions about the relationship of language to knowledge. The system of classical rhetoric was too powerful to be limited to the few forms of public speaking to which it was originally applied, and the questions about language and knowledge raised by classical rhetoricians were never to be put to rest. After the classical period, the bounds of rhetoric expanded, until today virtually all forms of discourse and symbolic communication can be included within its scope. Yet the classical system remained the basis of rhetoric throughout its history and in large measure remains so today.

CLASSICAL RHETORIC

Late in the fourth century B.C.E., Aristotle reduced the concerns of rhetoric to a system that thereafter served as its touchstone. To speak of classical rhetoric is thus to speak of Aristotle's system and its elaboration by Cicero and Quintilian.

Types of Rhetorical Discourse

In the classical system of rhetoric there are three principal kinds of public speech: the legal speech, which takes place in the courtroom and concerns judgment about a past action; the political speech in the legislative assembly, concerned with moving people to future action; and the ceremonial speech in a public forum, intended to strengthen shared beliefs about the present state of affairs. In the classical system, these three situations constitute the entire domain of rhetoric. Later rhetoricians expanded this list to include sermons, letters, and eventually all forms of discourse, even conversation, that could be seen as persuasive in intent.

Psychology and Audience Analysis

The rhetorical occasion always includes an audience, and the speaker must consider the motives that are likely to influence audiences of the three kinds of speech. Classical rhetoric thus examines the psychology and moral assumptions of the different kinds of people who may compose an audience. Aristotle assumes that people always seek to serve their own self-interest and that different kinds of people perceive their self-interest differently. Using these terms, he compares young men and old, the rich and the poor, and rulers of democracies and of oligarchies. He treats most psychological attributes as human nature, common to all people in all circumstances (young men have hot tempers and strong appetites, for example). Even for those attributes that are conditioned by social class, political interest, and history, he seeks the most general explanation. Audience analysis helps chiefly to determine the kinds of emotional appeals that might be used, for logical appeals (as we shall see) are not supposed to be subject to such vagaries.

The Preparation of a Speech

Classical rhetoric divides the process of preparing a persuasive speech into five stages:

1. Invention, the search for persuasive ways to present information and formulate arguments
2. Arrangement, the organization of the parts of a speech to ensure that all the means of persuasion are present and properly disposed
3. Style, the use of correct, appropriate, and striking language throughout the speech
4. Memory, the use of mnemonics and practice
5. Delivery, presenting the speech with effective gestures and vocal modulation

This five-part composing process remains a cornerstone of the study of rhetoric.

The speaker is supposed to produce a discourse by proceeding stepwise through the stages. Although the speaker's specific choices in each stage of the process depend on the occasion for his (or, rarely, her) speech, the five-part process is taken to be appropriate for composing any kind of speech. All of the parts are necessary to ensure that a full range of appeals is produced. The classical system assumes that there are three forms of persuasive appeal: to reason *(logos)*, to emotion *(pathos)*, and to the speaker's authority *(ethos)*. We shall see how these forms are included in a speech as we examine each stage of the process.

Invention. In the classical system, the first stage of composing, invention, is the most important, because here rational arguments — appeals to *logos* — are devised. Logical appeals are regarded as superior to the others. Aristotle assumes that human rationality is the most uniform and universal of the human mental abilities, or faculties, and so logical arguments will presumably have the widest currency. At the same time, he argues that emotional appeals are needed in the effective speech, though he and his successors lament the fact that rational appeals alone are not enough. Classical emphasis on *logos* is presented as if in recognition that human beings respond most strongly to rational appeals, though this idea may be more a hope than a fact, an attempt to increase the power of rational appeals by valorizing them.

Classical rhetoric offers several methods of generating rational appeals. One is to consider the common topics, or *topoi* (common places or *loci* in Latin), to see whether arguments can be developed in terms of any of them. The topics are stock formulas in which arguments may be cast. They include comparison and contrast, cause and effect, and argument a fortiori; they also include such seemingly non-rational appeals as puns on proper names. In addition to the universally applicable topics are special topics for particular kinds of speech or subject matter — the rules of evidence in criminal law, for example. When employing any of these heuristic devices, the rhetorician "invents" arguments in the sense of finding ways to combine and present evidence persuasively.

Rational appeals in classical invention are not designed to be equivalent to scientific demonstration. Aristotle draws an important distinction between demonstration, dialectic, and rhetoric and the type of knowledge found in each. Demonstration reveals unalterable truths about the physical world. Dialectic uses rigorous syllogistic logic to approach probable truths in questions about human affairs and philosophy that do not lend themselves to absolute certainty. Rhetoric also seeks probable truth in the realm of human affairs, relying on knowledge produced by demonstration and dialectic, along with traditional or received wisdom and the various means of finding persuasive connections, such as those suggested by the common topics.

Another form of rational appeal is the enthymeme, which, like the syllogism used in dialectic, deduces a conclusion from a general premise. But whereas the general premise of a syllogism is supposed to be true and its deduction therefore necessary, the general premise of an enthymeme is merely probable, leading to a tentative conclusion.

The rhetorician constructing an argument must draw on sources of knowledge that lie outside the domain of rhetoric. To ensure access to these sources, the rhetorician must be learned in philosophy, history, law, literature, and other fields of study, a point heavily stressed by Cicero and Quintilian. Given the scope of rhetoric, however, the distinctions between *inside* and *outside* can blur, and the nature of the rhetorician's activities with respect to knowledge can become unclear.

This problem is a continuing theme of rhetorical theory. In the classical view, rhetoric manages knowledge, conveying but not creating it; the rhetorician's activities are subordinate to the truth-seeking of the scientist and the philosopher. But it is by no means clear that philosophy or science has access to true knowledge. If, as some philosophers maintain, all knowledge is uncertain and constructed by argument, then rhetoric has the more value for its study of the ways in which argument and persuasion create conviction as well as for its role in creating the provisional agreements and shared values on which human community depends.

In Aristotle's day, the position that all knowledge is contingent was defended most ardently by the Sophists, who saw themselves as both philosophers and rhetoricians. In modern parlance, the Sophists treat rhetoric as epistemic, as making knowledge. Moreover, they tend to see all language use as rhetorical — persuasive in intent. That is, through language, people collectively construct a value-laden world view (the only kind of world view available) and reach agreement on how to act together for their mutual benefit in light of that world view. Different communities may see things differently because of their cultural traditions and historical circumstances. For the Sophists, there are no privileged nonrhetorical discourse and no privileged nonrhetorical knowledge.

The Sophists' position was attacked and discredited by Aristotle's teacher Plato. In traditional histories of rhetoric, the Sophists are often slighted, but their epistemic vision of rhetoric haunts the subject to the present day. Even Plato, who condemned the Sophists, came to see rhetoric as an essential component in the search for true knowledge. And in other eras the Sophistic view of rhetoric has reasserted itself. Today, philosophical skepticism about true or foundational knowledge has led interest in Sophism to emerge once more with renewed vigor.

Arrangement. In the stage of arrangement, the arguments devised through invention are placed in the most effective order. Aristotle says that all speeches have four parts: the introduction, the statement of the issue, the argument, and the conclusion. Logical appeals should go into the statement and argument, while appeals to *pathos* and *ethos* should appear in the introduction and conclusion. Cicero spells out a five-part structure with a more precise distribution of appeals: The introduction should contain ethical and pathetic appeals; the narration of the facts of the case, while ostensibly logical, should also be an occasion for pathetic appeals; the statement of position should hold the logical arguments in favor of the position; the refutation should make logical arguments against the opponent's position; and the conclusion should embody further pathetic and ethical appeals.

Emotional appeals are something of an embarrassment in the classical system. They are generated by a kind of invention process that examines the nature of emotions, the kinds of stimuli that may excite them, and the motives and inclinations of the different types of people to whom the emotional appeals might be directed. In the classical system, this process of formulating nonlogical appeals is distinguished from logical invention, and it shifts by default from the invention stage to the arrangement stage. In the arrangement stage, the speaker considers the kind of discourse to be presented, the nature of the subject, and the characteristics of the audience, all of which guide decisions about the relative weight and placement of logical and emotional appeals. Arrangement itself is thus a form of nonlogical appeal, as later rhetoricians acknowledged. From the seventeenth century on, philosophers paid increasing attention to psychology, which put both arrangement and emotional appeals on a new footing. Psychological theories offered a "natural" sequence of mental operations leading from reasoning to belief to action. Psychology also confirmed in new ways the classical observation that reason could rarely be persuasive by itself.

Style. Style is separated from invention and arrangement in the classical five-part scheme. It has the job of dressing up previously formulated ideas in attractive verbal garb. Aristotle tends to treat style as decoration, a sop to the base human desire for sensual enticements. Nevertheless, he begins what would become the habitual, not to say obsessive, practice among rhetoricians of cataloging and illustrating large numbers of verbal figures. Several times in its long history, the study of rhetoric has contracted to little more than the study of style. Rhetoric in the schools has often consisted of memorizing long lists of figures; stylistic rhetoric texts filled with such lists abounded, for example, in the Renaissance. Highly ornamented styles have often been valued for their beauty and ingenuity, and stylistic rhetoric came in time to be as closely allied with poetry as it was with oratory.

Stylistic rhetoric does not typically address the question of generating ideas, which is the province of invention. But for some rhetoricians, the search for effective figures is akin to an invention process. The rhetorical figures, like the topics of invention, can be seen as parallel to human thought processes. Hence, formulating ideas in figures and ornamenting arguments will make them structurally more understandable, memorable, and convincing. At the same time, the process of stylistic formulation can be seen as a heuristic method, in which ideas are discovered by the search for figurative expression. Metaphor in particular has been regarded as generative. The Sophists made this connection between style and generative thought and have been chastised for it; Renaissance stylistics would be denounced in turn. More recently, though, deconstructive critics have been working to rehabilitate this insight into the generative power of style.

The sensual power of word magic to create belief was perhaps most potently felt while rhetoric was still employed largely in oral genres, and response to this power may have dwindled as rhetoric increasingly moved to written forms. Certainly the last two stages of the five-part composing process, memory and delivery, dwindled in importance with the turn to print, though they did not disappear entirely.

Memory. Classical rhetoric adopted the notion that memory could be improved by treating it as a system of visualized locations, somewhat akin to the way the commonplaces are imagined to reside in actual mental locations that one tours during the invention process. The speaker memorizes the sequence of rooms in a building, assigns a vivid image to each section of the speech, and then associates the image with a location in the memorized building. Needless to say, this approach means memorizing two things rather than one, but there were those who found it workable.

For Plato, memory is a link not just with earthly places but with those heavenly places where ideal forms and true knowledge reside. The right method of cultivating memory, then, might give one access to these remote, transcendent realms of knowledge. Neoplatonists until well into the Renaissance sought to devise memory systems that would be sufficiently sensitive to the supposedly parallel structures of mind and world to facilitate the acquisition of vast amounts of new knowledge. Hence the presence of memory in the system of rhetoric raises in yet another form the question of how knowledge is represented in the mind.

Delivery. For Aristotle, delivery is an art akin to acting, which he despises. Like memory, delivery has often received rather perfunctory treatment, even by Quintilian and others who take a brighter view than Aristotle and acknowledge its importance. The Roman rhetoricians understand that voice, gestures, and facial expressions materially affect the impact of all that has gone into the composition of a speech. Delivery is a system of nonverbal signs with enormous power, a power recognized by eighteenth-century elocutionists and by twentieth-century electronic media analysts, among others.

The Influence of Classical Rhetoric

Rhetoric has frequently been treated as if it were chiefly a succession of reformulations of the classical system we have just outlined. There is some justice in this view. The fundamental concerns of rhetoric in all ages appear to be those defined in the classical period: purpose, audience, composing process, argumentation, organization, and style. Not only do the classical categories of rhetorical study persist, but so do many of the particulars. In every period we find discussions of the common and special topics, the steps in composing, the figures of speech, and so on. And with respect to larger questions of theory, the status of knowledge as true or contingent continues even today to be unsettled.

Yet for all the continuity of the rhetorical tradition, rhetoric has grown and changed. Classical rhetoric may name many of the fundamental concerns, but it does not exhaust the possibilities for understanding the nature of persuasive discourse, as a review of the history of rhetoric will suggest.

Late Classical Rhetoric in Rome

Roman rhetoricians (such as Cicero and Quintilian) draw largely on the Greeks (chiefly Gorgias, Plato, Isocrates, and Aristotle). Much of the work by the Roman writers is prescriptive, providing guidelines for employing the techniques arrayed in the five-part composing process. But Cicero and others also went beyond considerations of structure to speculate about the ways in which persuasion shaped belief and action. Oratory in Cicero's time (the first century B.C.E.) was a powerful political weapon — one Cicero himself wielded — and rhetoric, however derivative its theory, was an art that helped organize civilized communal life. By the time of Quintilian (the first century C.E.), Rome was an empire and political oratory was suppressed. Rhetoric became a form of entertainment, focused on stylistic extravagance. But Quintilian envisions the creation, through rhetorical training that includes broadly humane learning, of a "good man speaking well" who might save the state.

MEDIEVAL RHETORIC

Early Christianity

If Quintilian's good speaker were to be found in early medieval times, perhaps he would be a member of the new faith, Christianity. But many of the Church fathers doubted that pagan rhetoric could serve the needs of the new religion. They saw rhetoric as part of the hated Greco-Roman culture, imbued with the hopeless moral corruption of the pagan world. Moreover, whereas rhetorical invention generates probable knowledge through the commonplaces and the enthymeme, Christian knowledge is absolute. Similarly, whereas rhetoric (and classical philosophy generally) relies on reason to produce knowledge, Christian knowledge comes from revelation. Augustine, at the turn of the fifth century C.E., makes at last a practical decision in favor of rhetoric by focusing on the issue of persuasion: Christianity cannot afford to eschew a powerful tool for defending and expounding its principles and beliefs.

The Later Middle Ages

Augustine's accommodation of rhetoric and Christianity was not productive of much new work on rhetoric in the Middle Ages, however. Not long after Augustine's death, Boethius, one of the last scholars with classical training in Greek and Latin, wrote a brief summary of classical rhetoric. His summary, more widely available than the originals, reduced thousands of pages of theory and practical advice to a few lines on each of the most general points. This kind of work is typical of the treatment of rhetoric — and most other branches of learning — for almost eight hundred years after the times of Augustine and Boethius. Classical texts were rare, and the Church, while preserving them, also wished to preserve their rarity.

Rhetoric in the Middle Ages did produce sets of rules for the art of preaching and for the legal letters through which the far-flung Church and secular governments were administered. Manuals of preaching and of letter writing began to appear in great numbers after the twelfth century. Also persisting through the medieval period was the study of style, generally separated from other rhetorical concerns and associated with the composition of verse.

THE RENAISSANCE

Stylistic Rhetoric

The study of figures gave names to every sort of phrase and sentence, a practice that became more widespread in the fifteenth century. The emphasis on style was stimulated by renewed interest in classical learning, an interest exemplified in the letters by Italian humanist Laura Cereta. It was not possible, in the Renaissance, to speak without "using" rhetoric, and a great occupation of clever rhetors in this period was amplification of the names of figures and copious demonstrations of their use for the delectation of other experts. Many rhetorical terms, too, found their way into the new science of vernacular grammar: *colon, comma, apostrophe,* and *parenthesis*. For stylistic rhetoric texts in the Renaissance, the idea that all language use could be treated rhetorically was confined for the most part to style, to the forms of statements and not to the social situations of their utterance.

Private Discourse in Rhetoric

But the social situation of private discourse did enter the domain of rhetoric. Private discourse, however persuasive, had hitherto remained outside the boundaries of rhetoric; the art of letter writing, in the hands of the Renaissance humanists, grew to include private as well as public communications. Guides for letter writing, private conversation, and courtly etiquette, as can be seen in the work of Christine de Pisan, placed rhetoric at the site of considerable political power in a society increasingly governed by monarchs and their advisers.

Ramus

In the sixteenth century, the classical approach to rhetoric was attacked by the French philosopher Peter Ramus, who proposed a popular reform of the allied arts of dialectic and rhetoric. Dialectic sought to perfect the syllogism as a way of examining statements about the world. Logically perfect statements, as long as they were not inconsistent with divine revelation, were presumably true. Dialectic would thus grasp the truth (through the syllogism), while rhetoric would offer it to the public. Ramus, however, formally separates invention (and arrangement as well) from rhetoric and assigns it to dialectic. Ramus believes that there need not be overlap in contiguous fields of study, especially where one field possesses a clearly superior method — as in this case, where dialectic is, he says, superior. Rhetoric in Ramus's scheme is confined to style, memory, and delivery. Ramistic rhetoric, taken up almost entirely with matters of style, flourished well into the seventeenth century, though it was vigorously opposed by Ciceronians, who argued for the continued importance of all five parts of the classical composing process.

Science, Epistemology, and Rhetoric

The Ramist conception of dialectic was overturned by the inductive orientation of the new approach to science. Francis Bacon, at the turn of the seventeenth century, argues that the syllogism cannot discover anything new. The proper distinction to draw, Bacon says, is between inquiry, as the work of science, and recovery, as the work of rhetorical invention. Even though Bacon supports a rhetoric that includes all its traditional parts, one consequence of the new scientific movement of the seventeenth and early eighteenth centuries was the further estrangement of rhetoric from the source of knowledge. Some of Bacon's followers attack rhetoric as an unreliable tool for handling knowledge. And not only rhetoric but language itself comes under this attack.

But if language is unreliable, how is truth to be known? Can words and sentences, even if purged of ornament, stand for mental representations? Can language be purified for science or philosophy? Bacon addresses the problem this way: Human knowledge must be regarded as only a version of the objective truth, a version warped by prejudices, preconceptions, and imprecise language. Verbal representations of this knowledge introduce distortion because they are signs that may lose their definition, their link to the signified. Bacon hopes that careful observation and skeptical induction will overcome these epistomological limitations and reveal the truth of things, a truth that rhetoric may then disseminate. But by the very fact of elaborating the nature of mental and verbal "distortion," he reopens the possibility that the processes of thought and language are never neutral conveyors of truth.

THE ENLIGHTENMENT

John Locke also struggled with this problem. Human language must make use of generalizations, Locke contends, or else words will proliferate along with the multitude of things in the world until language becomes too cumbersome to use conveniently. Generalities don't actually exist: They are ideas, similarities perceived by human observers. But while Locke seems certain that the general idea comes first, he also suggests that the general idea is in some sense created by language. In any case, there is no guarantee that the generality signified by a word will convey the same idea to all speakers. This is a serious problem, and Locke and his successors blame rhetoric for making it worse. If only stylistic extravagance were curbed, they say, language might be closer to the things it names — if not to things out in the world, then at least to people's clear and distinct ideas about them.

For a number of seventeenth- and eighteenth-century rhetoricians, these complaints were a call for reform. Rhetoric was out of step with the times, it seemed, because invention relied on outdated deductive methods and stylistic rhetoric impeded the already-difficult search for truth. Rhetoric ought to moderate its reliance on the topics for invention, because those topics depend on received wisdom rather than observed fact. Furthermore, syllogistic reasoning should be limited, as in Bacon's scheme, to avoiding fallacies. And clearness (or "perspicuity") should of course be preferred to an ornamented style. These reforms proved to be widely influential and later allowed for the development of a more epistemologically sophisticated rhetoric.

The Eighteenth Century

Giambattista Vico, an Italian professor of rhetoric of the early eighteenth century, was one of the few in his day to challenge science's claim of epistemological superiority. Responding to the philosophy of René Descartes, Vico objects that the famous philosopher's method relies, no less than rhetoric does, on probability and belief rather than demonstration of absolute truth. Vico even sees rhetoric as superior to the Cartesian method, for rhetoric takes probability seriously, understands the ways in which argument produces belief, and trains young people for responsible civic action, as Cartesianism does not. An honest analysis of the function of language, Vico argues, will reveal the ways in which knowledge is actually formed, in contrast to the Cartesians' claims to have the real truth. Vico's ideas, however, had little influence in his own day. His elaboration of the epistemological doubts hinted at in Bacon conflicted with the positive thrust of the new theory of knowledge, a thrust that was supported by the growth of empirical scientific learning. Vico was seen as a reactionary, an opponent of scientific and philosophical progress.

But Bacon had already suggested an obvious and less contentious connection that rhetoric could make with epistemology, namely, through a new system of psychology. Rhetoric could observe the structure of the mind and thereby enhance communication. Rhetoric, after all, addresses the faculties of the mind. Should it not study the ways of making this address most efficient and effective? Moreover, by taking a scientific attitude toward the study of language, rhetoric could ally itself with a power that would otherwise remain a dangerous enemy. Thus, eighteenth-century rhetoricians endorse clarity as an ideal of style, support "natural" arrangement, and favor a rhetorical theory that follows "human nature" in appealing to reason and emotions. Moreover, they regard the classical authors as excellent observers of human nature. According to Locke's theory of uniform psychology, human nature presumably has not changed since the classical authors' day; therefore, studying these writers' works could not conflict with the new "scientific" standards of psychology.

Bacon identifies along with each mental faculty a particular genre that especially addresses it: philosophy for Reason, history for Memory, and literature for Imagination. George Campbell, writing late in the eighteenth century, extends Bacon's taxonomy of faculties and genres. Scientific demonstration is but one form of communication, says Campbell, appealing to one faculty, Reason, through a preferred style, perspicuity or clarity. Campbell even steers close to Vico's argument here, pointing out that demonstration relies on belief in previous demonstrations, proofs, and axioms. Between science and rhetoric, then, Campbell sees a range of probabilistic reasoning, not a difference in kind. Rhetoric will give the best account not only of reason but also of the other faculties of the human mind, Campbell argues, for rhetoric studies human sentiments, passions, dispositions, and purposes in order to affect them.

Though Bacon, Campbell, and others repeat the traditional definitions of occasions for oratory — at the bar, in the pulpit, and in the legislature — one effect of the psychological turn was to be the emphasis on "universal" modes of discourse, modes that address not audiences but mental faculties. Thus rhetoric moves toward a more "scientific" theory and takes a proprietary interest in psychology.

Rhetoric and Psychology

Psychology had been a concern for rhetoric since the time of Aristotle. Indeed, Aristotle has more care for psychology than most of his rhetorical descendants do. Most rhetorical systems focus on reasoning, discourse structures, and style but have little to say about appealing to a variety of audiences, beyond the rather obvious advice to adjust style and learning to their capacities. Ironically, perhaps, the new approach to psychology in the eighteenth century does not focus attention on audiences at all. Instead, it treats all minds as essentially the same. This approach conforms to Locke's influential idea of universal psychology, it is democratic (in the sense of being uniform, hence egalitarian), and it is expedient for an expanded theory of communication. The scene of psychological rhetoric, in its textbooks and theories, is a mind, not a public forum.

So closely connected were rhetoric and psychology by the nineteenth century that the influential psychologist Alexander Bain taught rhetoric and wrote a textbook on written composition. Bain argues that figures of speech reflect the mental operations of comparison, contrast, and association and that the modes of discourse — description, narration, exposition, argument, and poetry — correspond to mental faculties. For Bain, invention and arrangement are more or less determined by the nature of the modes of discourse: That is, description presents an object whose parts must be presented in some convenient order, narrative is the presentation of a chronological sequence of actions, and so on. For argument, invention is compounded of knowledge of the subject and syllogistic reasoning. As for style, clearness is still the standard, except, of course, for imaginative literature.

Psychology changed radically at the close of the nineteenth century, largely through the work of Sigmund Freud. The patient's speech is at the heart of psychoanalysis, but Freud and his followers were interested in what was hidden in this speech, in its source in nonverbal experiences and unconscious drives — not in its persuasive effects. Psychoanalysis pointed to mental realms apparently beyond the reach of verbal persuasion, and so rhetoric continued to rely for the structure of its appeals upon the older faculty psychology of Bain.

In the nineteenth century, too, the curricula of schools and colleges added a vast number of new subjects, responding at last to the demands of science, technology, and business, as well as the pressure for mass education. Rhetoric had had the lion's share of the curriculum, but competition from these other disciplines now forced rhetoric into one- or two-semester courses. Narrowed in compass, rhetoric focused more and more on written composition. Soon, composition became an adjunct of newly formed departments of English literature, and separate departments of speech communication arose to take over instruction in delivery and the study of rhetoric's history.

But if science, self, and society all escaped the domain of the rhetorical — at least for a time — they have been returning in recent times. In the late nineteenth century, philosopher and one-time rhetoric teacher Friedrich Nietzsche challenged the self-satisfied assumptions on which scientific knowledge appeared to its defenders to rest. What we are pleased to call Truth, says Nietzsche (echoing the Sophists), is a social arrangement, not a glimpse of ultimate reality. Scientists and philosophers delude themselves in thinking otherwise. They construct the world they wish to believe in, using a language that is far from objective and neutral. Language can never be so, says Nietzsche: It is always partial, value laden, intentional — in short, rhetorical. Nietzsche's ideas, so dissonant in his own time, have made their mark in ours.

THE TWENTIETH CENTURY

A number of twentieth-century rhetoricians have offered rhetorically grounded theories of meaning, value, intention, and knowledge. I. A. Richards, for example, sees in rhetoric an approach to meaning that can correct the "proper meaning fallacy" — the idea (already attacked by Nietzsche) that there is a direct link between words and the things or ideas they represent. Rhetoric shows, for Richards, that meaning is a function of context. Words are meaningful only in discourse (not, that is, in dictionaries), and discourse is meaningful to people who understand language by relating its present use to their previous experience of it. Richards thus defines rhetoric broadly, as the study of communication and understanding.

Kenneth Burke follows a similar path in his work. Discourse of all kinds, he says, seeks to motivate people in some way, so we should seek meaning in its intentions and effects. Language is a form of human action: It requires an agent with a purpose, a scene of action, a rhetorical strategy, and an actual speech or text. Seeing discourse this way, "dramatistically" as Burke calls it, is to see all language as motivated, hence as rhetorical. Burke also searches discourse for its ideological function of promoting identification with communities and their beliefs. In his analyses, rhetoric merges with political, psychological, sociological, religious, and aesthetic investigations of human behavior.

For Chaim Perelman, rhetoric is a powerful and necessary alternative to formal logic for the study of *practical* reasoning. Indeed, he says, formal logic is useless outside of its own tiny, abstract realm. Echoing Vico, Perelman objects to the Cartesian implication that probabilistic argument is not rational and therefore not worthy of development because it does not produce absolute truth. But probabilistic arguments are the basis of legal, ethical, and practical decisions that guide our lives. Rhetoric can tell us, says Perelman, about the way that knowledge and belief are formed by arguments based on probable reasoning, experience, and established custom. Moreover, a rhetorical view of knowledge serves as a warning against the claim, often advanced in illiberal causes, that some knowledge is absolute and beyond argument. Even in science, as modern philosophers of science admit (or at least debate), knowledge arises through argument within communities that share assumptions and beliefs.

Rhetorical theory, following these lines of development, has come to focus today on the question of the source and status of knowledge. Philosophers like Mikhail Bakhtin, Michel Foucault, Jacques Derrida, and Julia Kristeva, who do not work in the rhetorical tradition, nonetheless contribute to modern rhetorical theory through their important studies of language and its relation to knowledge. Foucault, for example, follows Nietzsche in attacking the idea that language is the passive conveyor of knowledge. Discourse, he says, is part of the network of knowledge and power, shaped by disciplines and institutions with their complex interactions and motivations. Authority to speak about certain kinds of knowledge (*ethos,* we might say) comes from institutional certification; reasoning is a function of accepted modes of reference and discipline-specific processes of validation; and the persistence of institutions and their prerogatives depends upon power that is maintained and exercised through discourse itself. In thus regarding language as intentional, powerful, caught up in the creation of knowledge and its uses, Foucault offers a theory that is entirely in line with the modern approach to rhetoric.

Concern about the status of knowledge and its relationship to language are by no means limited to the fields of rhetoric and philosophy. Scientific knowledge now appears to progress not by rational observation and the accumulation of facts but by argument. The unconscious mind is a kind of persuasive discourse, from the modern point of view, making psychoanalysis a form of rhetorical criticism. Such conclusions are echoed in virtually every field of knowledge: Our learning comes from interpretation, our disciplines grow by argument, our communities cohere through discourse, our ideologies are structures of persuasion; reality itself is a function of the way we use language.

The epistemic questions raised by the human sciences and even the natural sciences point to the need to study speech acts and speech genres, discursive formations and discourse communities, the dramatic scenes of communication, the linguistic construction of consciousness, and the rhetorical construction of knowledge. And indeed, this is the program put forward by the rhetoricians of our age. For rhetorical theory now, language is always persuasive in intent, always imbued with ethics and ideology. Language, as Richard Weaver puts it, is sermonic. It is not first a mental system but a social one, founded on dialogue, not linguistics. *Rhetoric* is synonymous with meaning, for meaning is in use and context, not words themselves. Knowledge and belief are products of persuasion, which seeks to make the arguable seem to be natural, to turn positions into premises — and it is rhetoric's responsibility to reveal these ideological operations. In examining its own ideological operations, rhetoric is looking to its own canon and its own exclusions, particularly of women and of Afro-Americans. These are the new concerns of rhetoric.

The epistemological and ideological orientation of rhetoric is not an entirely new development. Rhetoric has always been concerned with political action and the search for knowledge. The history of rhetoric is the story of a long struggle to understand the relationships between discourse and knowledge, communication and its effects, language and experience. Thus, the latest theories of rhetoric recover its earliest and most abiding concerns and build on a long tradition that is now, more than ever, worthy of our close attention.

Section Three: Definitions of Rhetoric

Section Three
Definitions of Rhetoric

The following are a variety of definitions that reveal the multifaceted and interdisciplinary function of rhetoric. Throughout our study we will find rhetoric to be an ever-evolving term that continues to be the subject of intense interest to students of communication.

rhet·o·ric (**rĕt'ər-ĭk**) *n.*
etymology—Greek/Latin—to believe/to urge

I. Dictionary Entries

***Webster's II New Riverside Dictionary* (1984)**

1. The art of expression; using language effectively and persuasively
2. The study of the elements, structure or style, used in writing and speaking.
3. Insincere or pretentious language that is vacuous such as campaign rhetoric.
4. Verbal communication; discourse.

***Oxford English Dictionary* (1910)**

The entry in the *OED* is, of course, quite long. Below, however, is the first definition along with a note that precedes the historical information for this meaning:

1. The art of using language so as to persuade or influence others; the body of rules to be observed by a speaker or writer in order that he may express himself with eloquence.

In the Middle Ages rhetoric was reckoned one of the seven 'liberal arts,' being comprised, with grammar and logic, in the 'trivium.'

***Greek-English Lexicon*, Liddell, Scott, Jones (1843; 1940)**

The modern English word *rhetoric* derives from the adjective of an elliptical phrase in classical Greek, *rhêtorikê* (*tekhnê*), which appears first in Plato's *Gorgias* (449a) and is usually translated as "the rhetorical art," or "the art of rhetoric." The Liddell, Scott, Jones *Greek-English Lexicon* shows that *rhêtorikê* belongs to a pair of words from the late fifth and early fourth centuries B.C.E. (e.g., in the texts of Plato, Isocrates, and Aristotle) that pertain to public speaking, or speaking about public matters: *rhêtoreia* ("oratory," or "public speaking") and *rhêtor* ("public speaker"). These words are related to a more ancient set of words that convey the more general meaning of that which is stated, specified, or proclaimed: *rhêma* ("that which is said" or "spoken"), *rhêtos* (something "stated," "covenanted"), and *rhêtra* (verbal agreement, covenant). This set of words derives, in turn, from *erô* ("I will say," "I will speak"), the future form of the verb *eirô* ("to say," "speak"; but also "to string together").

II. Definitions and Remarks from Philosophy and Rhetorical Theory

Gorgias, "Encomium on Helen" (414 B.C.E.)

The power of speech [*tou logou dunamis*] has the same effect on the condition of the soul as the application of drugs [*tôn pharmakôn*] to the state of bodies; for just as different drugs dispel different fluids from the body, and some bring an end to disease but others end life, so also some speeches [*tôn logôn*] cause pain, some pleasure, some fear; some instill courage, some drug and bewitch the soul with a kind of evil persuasion [*peithoi tini kakê*]. (Trans. George A. Kennedy [with additional interpolations of transliterated Greek])

Although Gorgias's "Helena" does not contain *rhetoric* or any cognate (and thus does not contain a definition of *rhetoric*), I begin the list with this passage because it provides an important example of the ancient Greek interest in persuasion (*peithô*) as the power of language over the mind.

Plato, *Gorgias* (c. 387–385 B.C.E.)

SOCRATES: In my opinion, then, Gorgias, it [i.e., rhetoric] is a certain pursuit that is not artful but belongs to a soul that is skilled at guessing, courageous, and terribly clever by nature at associating with human beings; and I call its chief point flattery. (463 a–b; trans. James H. Nichols, Jr.)

Plato, *Phaedrus* (c. 370 B.C.E.)

SOCRATES: Well, then, would not the rhetorical art taken as a whole be a certain leading of the soul [*psychagogia*] through speeches [*logon*], not only in law courts and whatever other public gatherings, but also in private ones, the same concerning both small and great things, and no less honored, with a view to what's correct at least, when it arises concerning serious than concerning paltry matters? (261a–b; trans. James H. Nichols, Jr.)

Aristotle, *On Rhetoric* (c. 360–c. 334 B.C.E.)

Rhetoric is an *antistrophos* to dialectic; for both are concerned with such things as are, to a certain extent, within the knowledge of all people and belong to no separately defined science. (1354a; trans. George A. Kennedy)

Isocrates, "Antidosis" (354–53 B.C.E.)

Speech (*logos*) is responsible for nearly all our inventions. It legislated in matters of justice and injustice and beauty and baseness, and without these laws, we could not live with one another. By it we refute the bad and praise the good; through it, we educate the ignorant and recognize the intelligent. We regard speaking well to be the clearest sign of a good mind, which it requires, and truthful, lawful, and just speech we consider the image (*eidolon*) of a good and faithful soul. With speech we fight over contentious matters, and we investigate the unknown. We use the same arguments by which we persuade others in our own deliberations; we call those able to speak in a crowd "rhetorical" (*rhêtorikoi*); we regard as sound advisers those who debate with themselves most skillfully about public affairs. If one must summarize the power of discourse, we will discover that nothing done prudently occurs without speech (*logos*), that speech is the leader of all thoughts and actions, and that the most intelligent people use it most of all. (15.255–57; trans. David C. Mirhady)

Cicero, *On Invention* (*De Inventione*, c. 87 B.C.E.)

There is a scientific system of politics [*Civilis quaedam ratio*] which includes many important departments. One of these departments—a large and important one—is eloquence [*eloquentia*] based on the rules of art, which they call rhetoric [*rhetorican*]. . . . Therefore we will classify oratorical ability [*oratoriam facultatem*] as a part of political science. (I.v.6; trans. H. M. Hubbell [interpolations added])

Cicero, *On the Orator* (*De Oratore*, 55 B.C.E.)

The duty of an orator is to speak in a style fitted to convince [*ad persuadendum accommodate*] (I.xxxi.137; 97; trans. E. W. Sutton and H. Rackham [interpolation added])

Quintilian, *Institutio Oratoria* (c. 95 C.E.)

Rhetoric is "the science of speaking well" [*rhetoricen esse bene dicendi scientiam*] (II.xv.38; trans. Donald A. Russell)

Francis Bacon, *The Advancement of Learning* (1605)

The duty and office of Rhetoric is, to apply Reason to Imagination for the better moving of the will. For we see Reason is disturbed in the administration thereof by three means; by Illaqueation or Sophism, which pertains to Logic; by Imagination or Impression, which pertains to Rhetoric; and by Passion or Affection, which pertains to Morality. (238)

John Locke, *An Essay Concerning Human Understanding* (1689)

. . . if we would speak of Things as they are, we must allow, that all the Art of Rhetorick, besides Order and Clearness, all the artificial and figurative application of Words Eloquence hath invented, are for nothing else but to insinuate wrong *Ideas*, move the Passions, and thereby mislead the Judgment; and so indeed are perfect cheats. . . . (Bk.III, ch. 10, § 34)

Giambattista Vico, *The Art of Rhetoric* (*Institutiones oratoriae, 1711–1741*)

Rhetoric or eloquence . . . is "the faculty of speaking appropriate to the purpose of persuading" (*facultas dicendi apposite ad persuadendum*). (5; trans. G. A. Pinton & A. W. Shippee)

George Campbell, *The Philosophy of Rhetoric* (1776)

In speaking there is always some end proposed, or some effect which the speaker intends to produce on the hearer. The word *eloquence* in its greatest latitude denotes, "That art of talent by which the discourse is adapted to its end" (Quintilian). (Bk. I, ch. 1)

Friedrich Nietzsche, "Description of Ancient Rhetoric" ("Darstellung der Antiken Rhetorik," 1872–73)

It is not difficult to prove that what is called "rhetorical," as a means of conscious art, had been active as a means of unconscious art in language and its development, indeed, that the *rhetorical is a further development,* guided by the clear light of the understanding *[Verstandes],* of *the artististic means which are already found in language.* (21)

I. A. Richards, *The Philosophy of Rhetoric* (1936)

Rhetoric, I shall urge, should be a study of misunderstanding and its remedies.

Kenneth Burke, *A Rhetoric of Motives* (1950)

Rhetoric is concerned with the state of Babel after the Fall. (23)

[Rhetoric] is rooted in an essential function of language itself, a function that is wholly realistic, and is continually born anew; the use of language as symbolic means of inducing cooperation in beings that by nature respond to symbols. (43)

Paolo Valesio, *Novantiqua: Rhetorics as a Contemporary Theory* (1980)

. . . rhetoric is the functional organization of discourse, within its social and cultural context, in all its aspects, exception made for its realization as a strictly formal metalanguage — in formal logic, mathematics, and in the sciences whose metalanguages share the same features. In other words: rhetoric is *all* of language, in its realization as discourse. (7)

Steven Mailloux, *Rhetorical Power* (1989)

. . . *rhetoric* [is] the political effectivity of trope and argument in culture. Such a working definition includes the two traditional meanings of rhetoric: figurative language and persuasive action. . . . (xii)

Jacques Derrida, "On Rhetoric and Composition: A Conversation" (1990)

... rhetoric, as such, depends on conditions that are not rhetorical. In rhetoric and speaking, the same sentence may have enormous effects or have no effects at all, depending on conditions that are not verbal or rhetorical. I think a self-conscious, trained teacher of rhetoric should teach precisely what are called "pragmatics"; that is, the effects of rhetoric don't depend only on the way you utter words, the way you use tropes, the way you compose. They depend on certain situations: political situations, economical situations—the libidinal situation, also. (15–16)

III. Definitions from Composition Studies

Wayne Booth, "The Rhetorical Stance" (1963)

The common ingredient that I find in all of the writing I admire (excluding for now novels, plays, and poems) is something that I shall reluctantly call the rhetorical stance, a stance which depends on discovering and maintaining in any writing situation a proper balance among the three elements that are at work in any communicative effort: the available arguments about the subject itself, the interests and peculiarities of the audience, and the voice, the implied character, of the speaker. I should like to suggest that it is this balance, this rhetorical stance, difficult as it is to describe, that is our main goal as teachers of rhetoric. (141)

Edward P. J. Corbett, "The Usefulness of Classical Rhetoric" (1963)

It might be objected that because classical rhetoric was confined to argumentative discourse it is too narrow a system for our composition courses. But there is no reason why many of the precepts of classical rhetoric cannot be used to guide students in writing the other three forms of discourse. Donald C. Bryant and Kenneth Burke have shown how classical rhetoric can be extended to cover expository writing, and Wayne C. Booth in his excellent book has shown us that there is a rhetoric of fiction too. A rhetoric of description could also be developed from a classical base. (164)

Francis Christensen, *Notes toward a New Rhetoric* (1967)

The hand-me-down rhetoric that we are trying to alter to fit the needs of our own times has three main divisions—invention, disposition, and style. . . .

In writing a piece of any length, one uses the resources of rhetoric in the order of their listing above—first invention, then disposition, and finally style. Although most rhetorics take up the divisions of their subject in this order, proceeding from the larger to the smaller units, it is an order that should not be allowed to dictate the order in which we take up these topics in teaching how to write. (x–xi)

Richard E. Young, Alton L. Becker, and Kenneth L. Pike, *Rhetoric: Discovery and Change* (1970)

. . . the discipline of rhetoric is primarily concerned with the control of a process. Mastering rhetoric means not only mastering a theory of how and why one communicates but mastering the process of communication as well. (9)

C. H. Knoblauch, "Modern Rhetorical Theory and Its Future Directions" (1985)

. . . rhetoric is the *process* of using language to organize experience and communicate it to others. It is also the *study* of how people use language to organize and communicate experience. The word denotes, as I use it, both a distinctive human activity and the "science" concerned with understanding that activity. All human beings are "rhetors" because they naturally conceive as well as share their knowledge of the world by means of discourse. Certain individuals are also "rhetoricians" because they study the nature, operations, and purposes of discourse. I suggest further that rhetoric, as a generic discipline, encompasses all forms of written as well as oral expression and includes the efforts of undeveloped speakers and writers as well as the achievements of literary artists. (29)

Section Four: Aristotle and Rhetoric

SECTION FOUR

Aristotle and Rhetoric

George Kennedy

A. ARISTOTLE'S LIFE AND WORKS

Aristotle tells us almost nothing about the events of his life, though he reveals his mind and values fully, especially in *Nicomachean Ethics*. What we know (or think probable) about the sequence of his activities and relationships with others derives from later sources, including a short biography and a long list of his works in *Lives of the Philosophers* (5.1–35) by Diogenes Laertius, probably written in the third century C.E. but derived from much earlier sources. The most important facts that contribute to an understanding of Aristotle's writings are his ties with the kings of Macedon, Philip and Alexander, and his association with Plato as a student and colleague for twenty years.[1]

Aristotle was born in Stagiros (later called Stagira) in northern Greece in 384 B.C.E. This was a Greek city but near the Macedonian kingdom, which was only partially Hellenized. Aristotle's father was a friend of and personal physician to the king of Macedon, and his mother, Phaestis, also came from a family of doctors. Aristotle probably spent some of his youth in Macedon, and he continued to have ties with the court, culminating forty years later in his being given responsibility for directing the education of the young prince who became Alexander the Great. His Macedonian connection rendered him somewhat suspect to Athenians in later life. Aristotle's own education had probably included the usual study of language, poetry, music, and geometry, as well as athletic training in the gymnasium. A few references (e.g., *Rhetoric* 1.11.15) suggest that as a young man he had particularly enjoyed hunting with dogs. His father died when Aristotle was quite young, but the family's connections with medicine may have been a source of his unusual interest in biology and his inclination to see change in terms of organic development.

After Aristotle's father's death a man named Proxenus, probably a relative, became his guardian and in 367 B.C.E. arranged for Aristotle to go to Athens and to become a student-member of the Academy, a center for advanced studies in philosophy and science that Plato had established in the outskirts of the city.[2] This was a sign of an early serious interest in philosophy. By this time Aristotle had doubtless read Plato's early Socratic dialogues, as well as *Gorgias*, with its criticism of sophistic rhetoric, and *Republic*, Plato's search for understanding of justice by imagining the creation of an ideal city where philosophers would be kings. As it happened, Plato was not present in Athens during the first few years of Aristotle's residence there, for he had gone to Sicily in a vain attempt to help create an ideal kingdom in Syracuse. During Plato's absence the intellectual life of the Academy went on, probably under the direction of the mathematician and astronomer Eudoxus and Heracleides Ponticus, a scientist and historian. Aristotle would have participated in symposia and dialectical disputes and attended occasional lectures, as well as pursued research projects of his own. His major project came to involve developing a theory of logical argument, which was to lead to the composition of works called *Categories* and *Topics*. He would also have experienced the cultural and political life of the Athenian democracy, attending plays in the theater and perhaps listening to debates in the Assembly, which probably gave him his first experience of political oratory.

Plato returned to Athens in 365 B.C.E., and it was probably between 365 and 361 (when he again went to Syracuse for two years) that his personal influence on Aristotle was its greatest. Aristotle retained throughout his life personal affection for Plato and learned much from him, but his instinctive feeling for philosophy came to be far more pragmatic than Platonic idealism. Whatever his initial attitude, Aristotle eventually rejected some fundamental Platonic concepts, such as the reality of transcendent ideas. In particular, the Forms of the Good, the Beautiful, and the True—which Plato accorded the status of the only absolute reality—were to Aristotle not independent entities but abstractions created by the human mind.[3] His interest in political theory clearly developed out of Plato's work but again was more pragmatic, based on study of existing constitutions in their historical development and defining the checks and balances that might create stability in a mixed constitution rather than seeking to imagine an ideal state. Though conventionally pious, Aristotle preferred to live in the real world and was curious about almost all its details. Although he always shared many of Plato's ethical values, his theory of ethics is not based on religious belief of reward and punishment in the afterlife (as was Plato's) but on how to achieve happiness in a secular society by rational control of the emotions.

The writings of Aristotle that survive in complete form, including *On Rhetoric*, are treatises—systematic expositions of subjects which he probably sometimes used as notes for lectures. They were not published—that is, multiple copies were not made for sale in bookstores—but were kept in his own library for his use and revision and probably for study by others. They are therefore known as his "esoteric" works. This status probably explains their lack of literary polish. We may be allowed to hope that when he used the texts for lecture notes Aristotle expanded and illustrated what he said and perhaps even entertained questions. Although the Aristotelian corpus —the collected esoteric works—was regarded by the philosophers of later antiquity and the medieval scholastic philosophers as constituting a single consistent system of thought, inconsistencies in terminology and even in doctrine indicate that most of the texts as we read them now, including *On Rhetoric*, represent a development of Aristotle's thinking over many years with repeated revision and additions to the texts. The nature and extent of this development in each area of Aristotle's thought is a controversial subject much discussed by modern students of Aristotelian philosophy.[4] In writing systematic accounts of philosophy Aristotle departed from the model of Plato who, like his teacher, Socrates, favored dialogue over lectures as a teaching method and resisted authoritative written statements of philosophical doctrines.[5]

Aristotle also published some works, mostly in the form of dialogues, especially during the years he was a member of the Academy and under the eye of Plato. These were read in antiquity and admired for their style as well as for their arguments. They did not survive the devastations of later antiquity and are known today only from quotations, abstracts, and allusions by others. The dialogues included *On the Poets*, which probably anticipated some of the ideas found in the *Poetics*, and a dialogue on rhetoric, entitled *Gryllus*, named after the son of the historian Xenophon whose death in battle in 363 B.C.E. had evoked a series of eulogies.[6] According to the Roman rhetorician Quintilian (2.17.14), it contained an argument that rhetoric is not an "art," reminiscent of Socrates' claim in Plato's *Gorgias*; this could also be read as a criticism of Isocratean epideictic. Since the work was in dialogue form, it is apt to have argued both sides of the question and thus may have anticipated some of the ideas in *On Rhetoric*,[7] for in that later work Aristotle unhesitatingly regards rhetoric as an art (1.1.2).

This change was perhaps a result of a more thorough consideration of the nature of rhetoric. Sometime in the mid-350s B.C.E., now a senior member of the Academy, Aristotle is said to have begun to offer a course on rhetoric.[8] Our information comes from much later sources and may not be entirely reliable, but the course seems to have been open to the general public—offered in the afternoons as a kind of extension division of the Academy and accompanied by practical exercises in debate. According to the reports, a reason for offering the course was a desire to counteract the influence of Isocrates, whose school was the Academy's main competitor and rival. Isocrates was teaching his own form of sophistic rhetoric, which he called "philosophy," to numbers of students from Athens and abroad.

We do not know whether Aristotle was asked by Plato to undertake this teaching or whether it was his own idea. Although not an Athenian and thus with limited personal experience of civic oratory, Aristotle's interest in logical argument led easily into consideration of public argumentation. Isocrates' defense of his teachings in the *Antidosis* dates from 353 B.C.E. and may represent, at least in part, his own reaction to Aristotle's teaching. (See Appendix I.E.2 at the end of this book.) Some of the text of *On Rhetoric* as we read it today probably is a revision of what was said in the "afternoon" lectures. That would include much of Book 1 (except for the two opening chapters) and probably much of the discussion of style and arrangement in the second half of Book 3. The reasons for believing that these chapters date from an early period include the presence of practical advice about what to say in a speech, the presence of some philosophical views known to have been current in the Academy but inconsistent with those Aristotle held later, the absence of cross-references (except for a few that could easily have been inserted later) to other treatises of Aristotle, and numerous historical references to events and people of the 350s.[9] In what we can see of the early lectures, Aristotle seems to be developing a system of rhetoric along the lines proposed by Plato in *Phaedrus*, emphasizing the importance of knowledge of the subjects to be discussed and of logical argument, though he probably had not yet developed his theory of the enthymeme and of the role of *ēthos* and *pathos* in oratory. It was probably in preparing to teach rhetoric that Aristotle compiled, or had assistants compile, the *Synagōgē tekhnōn*, a survey of the rhetorical doctrines found in handbooks of the fifth and fourth centuries. We shall return in the next section to the relationship of Aristotle's views of rhetoric to what was found in the handbooks and to the teachings of Isocrates and Plato.

Although Aristotle was recognized in the Academy as potentially the ablest of the followers of Plato, since he was not an Athenian he could not succeed him as Scholarch (head of the school), a position which went to Plato's nephew, Speusippus. Thus in 347 B.C.E., in anticipation of or soon after the death of Plato, Aristotle left Athens and went first to Assos in Asia Minor and then to the island of Lesbos, where he did much of his biological research and where his most famous pupil, Theophrastus, joined him. Then in 343 or 342 King Philip persuaded him to come to Macedon as tutor to Alexander, about thirteen years old at this time. Aristotle probably offered him instruction in logic, literature, rhetoric, political theory, and ethics. A letter from Isocrates to Alexander that was enclosed in a letter to Philip praises the young man for studying rhetoric but expresses carefully worded reservations about exercises in dialectic, which would certainly have been part of Aristotle's instruction.[10] Isocrates never mentions either Plato or Aristotle by name in any of his writings.[11] Aristotle probably revised his earlier lectures on rhetoric and somewhat adapted them to Alexander's potential needs, including adding references to Isocrates' speech *Philippus*, addressed to Alexander's father and doubtless of great interest at the Macedonian court. This speech was completed in 346, so Aristotle's references must have been added after that date.

Aristotle's work with Alexander ended by 340 B.C.E. From then until 335 he was probably living in Macedon or Stagiros and continuing philosophical research with a few private students. He apparently worked on a revision of his notes on rhetoric at this time, for it contains references to historical events of the period. In 338 Philip defeated the Athenians and their allies at the Battle of Chaeronea, ending the political significance of the Greek city states in the ancient world (though Athens remained a cultural center, a kind of university town, for centuries). In 336 Philip was assassinated and Alexander succeeded to the throne. In 335 Aristotle returned to Athens and opened his own school there in the *peripatos* ("colonnade," thus the name "Peripatetic" school) of the gymnasium of the Lyceum, not far from where the Hilton Hotel now stands. In the gymnasium, or nearby, were a library, study rooms, and a dining room where he could meet with students and friends for symposia.[12] Whereas Plato's Academy was a residential community in an ideal rustic setting, Aristotle's students found their own housing in the busy city.

It seems possible that Aristotle had long been hoping to return to Athens and that he had been preparing to teach popular subjects, including rhetoric, politics, ethics, and poetics, as a way of attracting students. We do not, however, have any specific testimony that Aristotle actually used the text of *On Rhetoric* as a basis for lectures at this time, and he eventually turned his attention to the more abstruse subject of metaphysics. On the death of Alexander in 323 B.C.E., when anti-Macedonian sentiment was strong in Athens, Aristotle turned his school over to Theophrastus and went to live in Chalcis on the island of Euboea, which was the original home of his mother's family. He died there in 322.

Although probably not a wealthy man, Aristotle seems to have had adequate resources to finance his school and research. Plato had not charged tuition of his students; Isocrates did and Aristotle may have done so as well. Diogenes Laertius, drawing on earlier sources, preserves Aristotle's will and a brief personal description of his appearance in later life. According to this Aristotle had thin legs, was partially bald, liked to wear rings, and spoke with a lisp. He was married, had one daughter, and, after his wife's death, fathered a son, Nicomachus, by a concubine. For the subsequent history of his library, including the text of *On Rhetoric*, see Appendix II.B.

B. RHETORIC BEFORE ARISTOTLE

Rhetoric, in the most general sense, can be regarded as a form of mental or emotional energy imparted to a communication to affect a situation in the interest of the speaker. Help! HELP! **HELP!** utilizes simple rhetorical devices—repetition (a figure of speech) and pitch and volume (features of delivery)—to convey a message whose intent and energy are compelling.

So understood, rhetoric is a feature of all human communication, even of animal communication. Traditional nonliterate societies all over the world—the aboriginal Australians are a good example—use a variety of rhetorical devices in their deliberations and have terms to describe rhetorical genres and procedures. Even when thought of as the theory and practice of public address in a literate society rhetoric is not solely a western phenomenon. The earliest known rhetorical handbook is *The Instructions of Ptahhotep*, composed by an Egyptian official sometime before 2000 B.C.E.; it gives advice about how to speak and when to keep silent if brought before a judge or ruler. Some of what is said resembles precepts in the Old Testament, as in Psalm 16: "Pleasant speech increases persuasiveness. . . . Pleasant words are like a honeycomb, sweetness to the soul and health to the body." There is an extensive rhetorical literature, both collections of speeches and writing about rhetoric, from ancient China and India. These matters are discussed, with examples and bibliography, in a book entitled *Comparative Rhetoric* (Kennedy 1998).

The earliest surviving work of Greek literature is the *Iliad*, traditionally attributed to a nebulous figure named Homer who perhaps lived about seven hundred years before Christ. It originated as part of a cycle of oral epic poems and was written down by scribes after the introduction of the alphabet in the Greek-speaking world, achieving its present form by around 550 B.C.E. The *Iliad* and its companion poem, the *Odyssey*, place a high value on eloquent speech, almost equal to military prowess, and contain many poetic versions of debates and speeches that already utilize features of argument, arrangement, and style later described in rhetorical handbooks (Kennedy 1999:5–12). Aristotle sometimes quotes the *Iliad*, other early poetry, and speeches in Greek tragedy to illustrate rhetorical practice. The important role of public address in Greece in the two centuries before Aristotle is well illustrated by the numerous speeches that the historians Herodotus,

Thucydides, and Xenophon included in their works. These speeches are reconstructions of what may have been said, but many examples of actual Greek speeches survive, the works of the Attic Orators of the late fifth and fourth centuries B.C.E. The most famous of these orators are Antiphon, Lysias, Isocrates, Aeschines, and Demosthenes. Aristotle could have read some of their speeches and may have heard other speeches when they were first delivered. Modern students beginning their study of the history of rhetoric should read some Greek speeches in English translation in order to better understand the context of Aristotle's rhetorical theories. Appendix I contains translations of Lysias' speech *Against the Grain Dealers*, an example of a speech given in a court of law, and of Demosthenes' *Third Philippic*, an example of a speech given in the Athenian Assembly. The most famous speech given in Aristotle's lifetime is Demosthenes' defense of his policies in resisting Philip of Macedon, known as *On the Crown* and delivered in 330. Aristotle may have heard it, but he does not mention Demosthenes' orations. His sympathies, of course, were with Philip and Macedon.

The English word "rhetoric," and its various forms in European languages, is derived from the Greek world *rhētōr*, a speaker, especially a speaker in a public meeting or court of law, sometimes equivalent to what we might call a "politician." The first datable appearance of the abstract noun *rhētorikē*, meaning the art of a public speaker, occurs in Plato's dialogue *Gorgias* (448d9), probably written around 380 B.C.E., where Socrates mentions "what is called rhetoric" and Gorgias acknowledges that this is what he teaches. This suggests the currency of the word "rhetoric" in Athens by the dramatic date of that dialogue, sometime in the last quarter of the fifth century, and in any event the word, a derivative of *rhētōr*, would have been easily understood by a speaker of Greek. Its use by Plato and Aristotle established it as a distinct area of study and eventually part of the curriculum of the liberal arts. Before and after "rhetoric" came into use there were other terms current. One was *peithō*, which means "persuasion"; more common was use of the word *logos*, meaning word or speech, in combination with other words: a *dēmiourgos logōn* was a "worker of words," and thus an orator; *tekhnē logōn*, "art of words," was used to describe the technique or art of speech and became the common title for a handbook of public speaking.

The art of rhetoric as studied in modern times had its birth in Greece, and, though it shared many features with rhetoric in non-western society, it has also had distinctive qualities that differentiate it culturally from other traditions. These qualities are closely connected with the development of democracy in Athens and some other Greek cities. The Greeks, already as seen in the *Iliad*, were a highly argumentative, contentious people; their city states were almost constantly at war with each other, and in times of peace they turned their energies into competitive athletics. Their rivalries and arguments contrast with values commonly found in Middle Eastern and Far Eastern cultures, where strong central governments discouraged or prevented public debate (and where organized athletics did not develop). Under democratic governments in Athens and some other Greek cities in the fifth and fourth centuries B.C.E., all important decisions about public policy and actions were made after debate in an assembly of the adult, male citizens, any one of whom could speak. Chaos could easily have resulted, but in order to arrive at some closure and avoid fighting, the Greeks invented the practice of deciding issues by vote of the majority, something unique to the democratic process. The Athenian law courts were also remarkably democratic. Both criminal and civil cases were heard before large juries, sometimes a thousand or more jurors, chosen by lot from the male citizens. Since there were no professional lawyers and no public prosecutors, criminal prosecutions had to be brought by an interested party, defendants were ordinarily expected to deliver one or more speeches on their own behalf, and prosecution and defense in civil cases similarly demanded an ability to address the jury in person in a set speech. In order to help litigants effectively plan and present a case, handbooks of judicial rhetoric were written and could be bought for a modest sum.

The earliest of these was apparently composed by a Sicilian named Tisias, called Corax, or the "Crow," sometime around 460 B.C.E.[13] Copies of it were brought to Athens and other, more extensive handbooks were written there. In *Phaedrus* (266d–267d) Plato gives a brief, somewhat belittling, survey of them, showing that they were organized around the conventional parts of a judicial oration: prooemion, narration, proof, and epilogue. Examples of what to say were given and could be adapted to actual situations. In connection with his earliest teaching of rhetoric around 355 Aristotle compiled a work in two books entitled *Synagōgē tekhnōn*, or "Collection of the Arts," which summarized the teaching of each of the handbooks known to him. He found them lacking in most respects and repeatedly criticizes them in *On Rhetoric* (e.g., 1.1.9; 3.13.3). They were, he complains, concerned only with judicial rhetoric and its parts and neglected deliberative oratory, a finer genre, and they gave too much attention to arousing emotions to the neglect of logical argument. In Appendix II.A, at the end of this volume, can be found a more detailed account of "The Earliest Rhetorical Handbooks," together with documentation and bibliography.

A second influence on the development of rhetorical teaching in Greece against which Plato and Aristotle reacted was that of the sophists. Among the most famous were Protagoras, Gorgias, and Hippias. A sophist was a teacher, often a foreigner who had come to Athens, who promised to provide practical verbal skills to students for a fee. Although some of the sophists made use of the question-and-answer method of instruction adopted by Socrates,[14] their more characteristic teaching technique, whatever the subject chosen, was *epideixis*, a demonstrative speech, long or short, often flamboyant, in which the sophist undertook to demonstrate some proposition artistically. Sometimes myth or allegory was employed; sometimes the argument was an indirect one in which all possibilities were enumerated, all but one disposed of, and the last accepted as valid. Sometimes the audience was asked to choose the form of the sophist's demonstration.[15] Among surviving examples of sophistic *epideixis* are speeches in Plato's *Phaedrus*,[16] Gorgias' *Encomium of Helen* (English translation in Appendix I.A) and *Palamedes*, the *Ajax* and *Odysseus* of Antisthenes, and the *Odysseus* of Alcidamas. All of these can be read as illustrating methods of speech. They make use of logical and stylistic devices that could be imitated by students, and some pretend to be addressed to a jury in a court of law. Sophistic instruction was largely oral, but such speeches could be copied down and serve as examples of oratory to be studied or imitated or quarried for commonplaces by the sophist's pupils, who could thus acquire not only the master's theory of oratorical partition, but also his techniques of argument, features of his style, and perhaps something of his delivery, all parts of later rhetorical teaching. We see this system of learning in practice in the opening pages of Plato's *Phaedrus*. The young Phaedrus has much admired a sophistic speech by Lysias,[17] secured the autograph (228a–b), and is trying to memorize it when he encounters Socrates, who shows him how to compose a speech on the same theme that will be better in structure and argument, and later delivers a speech on the opposite side of the issue. Speeches of this type are to be distinguished from serious expositions of an idea by a sophist, some of whom deserve to be regarded as philosophers: Prodicus' "Choice of Heracles," for example, which is a moral allegory, or Alcidamas' "On Those Writing Written Speeches," or the rhetorical pamphlets of Isocrates. In these works the subject matter definitely counted very much; in the former, more sophistic type, it was a way of holding the audience's attention while demonstrating a method. Some sophistic *epideixis*, of course, fell in between these extremes. Gorgias' *Helen* (of which a translation can be found in Appendix I.A) illustrates a method and expounds some serious ideas about the nature of speech and human psychology, but at the end he refers to the speech as a *paignion*, or "plaything." In the surviving works of Athenian orators of the fifth and fourth centuries B.C.E. only the three tetralogies attributed to Antiphon are certainly to be regarded as having been written to furnish models of oratory. They do not refer to specific occasions and are excellent illustrations of argument. For actual courtroom use their arguments could be adapted by introduction of documents and witnesses, by development of commonplaces, and by combination of sources. There was, thus, no reason why collections of examples of argument or style should consist of complete speeches. We read that collections of introductions and conclusions were made by Antiphon, Critias, Cephalus, and Thrasymachus,[18] and the works of Demosthenes contain a collection of prooemia for political speeches.

A crucial passage for understanding how rhetorical technique was taught by a leading sophist is what Aristotle says at the end of his short treatise on *Sophistical Refutations* (183b16–184b7). Aristotle was trying to create a theoretical and systematic art of dialectic to replace an unscientific sophistic eristic;[19] the beginning is difficult, he says (183b23), but once started, progress will be made, as has been the case in rhetorical studies (*tous rhētorikous logous*) with a succession of writers leading from Tisias,[20] to Thrasymachus, Theodorus, and others. With this he contrasts (183b36) the educational technique of the sophist Gorgias in which, he says, students were assigned ready-made speeches to memorize, "as though a shoemaker were to try to teach his art by presenting his apprentice with an assortment of shoes." In Plato's dialogue *Gorgias* (449b), Gorgias claims to be able to make people into *rhētores* like himself, but as he appears in both Plato and Aristotle he lacks the ability to conceptualize his views of rhetoric. His students were expected to learn by imitation; perhaps he offered some criticism of their efforts. Gorgias did publish prose works other than speeches, including a treatise that seeks to prove that nothing exists, that if it did exist it could not be apprehended by human beings, and if it were apprehended by someone knowledge of it could not be communicated to another.[21] But the references to his statements about rhetoric do not seem to include a judicial handbook like those described earlier.[22]

Isocrates (436–338 B.C.E.) was the most influential teacher of rhetoric in Aristotle's time. Around 390, before Plato created the Academy, Isocrates opened a school in Athens to train future leaders of Greek society in the skills of civic life, especially speech; it attracted a large number of students from Athens and abroad and continued in existence for fifty years. He had probably been a student of Gorgias. The method of his school resembled the teaching of Gorgias and other sophists in that he composed speeches for students to imitate, but he probably also lectured on rhetoric, using his own speeches as examples of method, and since he had come under the influence of Socrates, he presents his teaching as "philosophy" (see the selection from *Against the Sophists* in Appendix I.E.1). In his own way, Isocrates sought to answer one criticism of rhetoric attributed to Socrates in Plato's *Gorgias* by proposing a special subject matter for rhetoric: not speeches in legal disputes, but the great issues of Greek society and its historical tradition, especially the need for the union of the Greek states against threats from Persia. By composing speeches on such themes (as described in his *Antidosis* and elsewhere), he sought to condition students' moral behavior so that they would think and speak noble, virtuous ideas and implement them in civic policy, thus providing a response to claims that rhetoric was an art of deception and flattery. His own speeches were not delivered in public but published as pamphlets. Aristotle had clearly read them, quotes examples of rhetorical technique from them, and largely refrains from criticism of Isocrates in *On Rhetoric*. Later sources, however, record a tradition of hostility between the two men. Isocrates' school was in direct competition with the Academy of Plato, and when Aristotle first taught rhetoric in the Academy in the 350s he is said to have been motivated by opposition to Isocrates' teaching.[23] The most evident difference between Aristotelian and Isocratean teaching is the great emphasis put on truth, knowledge of a subject, and logical argument by Aristotle in contrast to Isocrates' inclination to gloss over historical facts and his obsession with techniques of amplification and smoothness of style. Aristotle doubtless thought that Isocrates was at heart a sophist, that his philosophy was shallow, and that as a teacher of rhetoric he failed to give his students an adequate understanding of logical argument—which many at the time regarded as tiresome verbal pedantry.[24] Although Aristotle quotes Isocrates' speeches repeatedly, and although they both had close connections with the Macedonian court, it seems clear that Aristotle retained his early objections to Isocrates as a rhetorician (see, e.g., *On Rhetoric* 1.9.38). It has become a commonplace of the history of rhetoric to speak of two traditions: the Aristotelian, which stresses the logical side of the subject, and the Isocratean, emphasizing the literary aspects of rhetoric.[25]

The influence of Plato (429–347 B.C.E.) on Aristotle's view of rhetoric is strong but complex. As Plato describes in his *Seventh Epistle*, he had been embittered against contemporary rhetoric by his own frustrated attempts to participate in politics and by the trial and execution of his master, Socrates, at the hands of the Athenian democracy in 399. His criticism is most shrill in the dialogue *Gorgias*, completed about the time Aristotle was born. In the first two parts of the dialogue (the conversations of Socrates with Gorgias and Polus), the existence of any valid art of rhetoric is called into question, though some of what is said is ironic or deliberately provocative on Socrates' part. This is true of Socrates' argument, found in Appendix I.B, that since a rhetorician "knows" justice he must necessarily always be just, and his analogy between rhetoric and cookery as sham arts of flattery. Socrates demands that rhetoric have some subject matter particular to itself, but none of the possibilities (e.g., politics or justice) satisfy him. As noted in the first section of this introduction, Aristotle's early work, the dialogue *Gryllus*, contained arguments that rhetoric was not an "art," that is, not something capable of being reduced to a system. However, Aristotle's study of dialectic led him to realize that rhetoric, like dialectic, was an art, capable of systematic description, which differed from most other arts and disciplines in teaching a method of persuasion that could be applied to many different subject matters. Plato himself had led the way to the development of a philosophical rhetoric in a passage toward the end of *Gorgias* (504e):

> Will not the orator, artist and good man that he is, look to justice and temperance? And will he not apply his words to the souls of those to whom he speaks, and his actions too, and . . . will he not do it with his mind always on this purpose: how justice may come into being in the souls of the citizens and how injustice may be removed, and how temperance may be engendered and intemperance removed, and every other virtue be brought in and vice depart?

In Plato's *Phaedrus*, written ten years or more after *Gorgias*, Socrates is made to develop the possibility of this ideal, philosophical rhetoric—something quite different from that flourishing in Greece or that taught by Isocrates. Near the end of the dialogue (277b5–c6) he summarizes what he has been saying as follows:

> Until someone knows the truth of each thing about which he speaks or writes and is able to define everything in its own genus, and having defined it knows how to break the genus down into species and subspecies to the point of indivisibility, discerning the nature of the soul in accordance with the same method, while discovering the logical category which fits with each nature, and until in a similar way he composes and adorns speech, furnishing variegated and complex speech to a variegated soul and simple speech to a simple soul—not until then will it be possible for speech to exist in an artistic form in so far as the nature of speech is capable of such treatment, neither for instruction nor for persuasion, as has been shown by our entire past discussion.

This ideal rhetoric, intended primarily for one-to-one communication, is clearly highly unrealistic if applied to public address, where the audience is made up of a variety of "souls" with differing patience and grasp of detailed argument. What Aristotle does in *On Rhetoric* is adapt the principles of Plato's philosophical rhetoric to more realistic situations. A speaker, he says (1.1.12), should not seek to persuade the audience of what is "debased." He posits three modes of persuasion that are an adaptation of Plato's call for fitting the speech to the souls of the audience (1.2.3). These become Aristotle's *ēthos*, or the projection of the character of the speaker as trustworthy; *pathos*, or consideration of the emotions of people in the audience; and *logos*, inductive and deductive logical argument. He seeks to provide a speaker with a basis for argument in "truth": that is, in knowledge of the propositions of politics and ethics and of how to use this knowledge to construct arguments (1.5–14, 2.18–26). He also supplies an understanding of psychology (2.1–11) and advice about adapting a speech to the character of an audience, viewed as types (2.12–17). His response to Plato on the subject of rhetoric (though without naming him) is analogous to his responses on the subject of the value of poetry, the nature of politics, ethics, and other subjects—less idealistic and more pragmatic, but based on philosophical values and methods.

C. ARISTOTLE'S CLASSIFICATION OF RHETORIC

Aristotle was the first person to give serious consideration to drawing a map of learning and to defining the relationship between the various disciplines of the arts and sciences, which were emerging as separate studies for the first time in the fourth century B.C.E. Aristotle's map of learning is the ultimate ancestor of library catalogues and the organization of the modern university in departments of arts and sciences. His own scheme can be found in Book 6 of *Metaphysics*, in Book 6 of *Nicomachean Ethics*, and in passing references elsewhere.

Aristotle divided intellectual activity into (1) theoretical sciences, where the goal is "knowing," knowledge for knowledge's sake, and which include mathematics, physics, biology, and theology; (2) practical arts, where the goal is "doing" something, including politics and ethics; and (3) productive arts of "making" something, including architecture, the fine arts, the crafts, and also medicine (which produces health). In addition, there are (4) methods or tools (*organa*), applicable to all study but with no distinct subject matter of their own. Logic and dialectic belong in that class. Aristotelian scholars of late antiquity and the Middle Ages regarded rhetoric as one of these methods or tools, largely on the basis of what is said in *On Rhetoric* 1.1. Modern scholars have tended to attribute to Aristotle the view that rhetoric is a productive art, like poetics. What he actually says in 1.2.7, however, is that rhetoric is a mixture. It is partly a method (like dialectic) with no special subject of its own, but partly a practical art derived from ethics and politics on the basis of its conventional uses. In *Nicomachean Ethics* 1.2.4–6 he calls rhetoric a part of the architectonic subject of politics. In defining rhetoric in *On Rhetoric* 1.2.1, however, he says that it is an ability of "seeing" the available means of persuasion (thus not necessarily using them oneself) and employs a verb related to the word *theory*. Thus, rhetoric in Aristotle's view also has a theoretical element and in addition clearly does often "produce" persuasion, speeches, and texts. In reading *On Rhetoric* we perceive a gradual shift of focus, moving from the use of rhetoric as a tool (like dialectic) in 1.1 to its theoretical aspects in 1.2, its political and ethical content in the rest of Books 1 and 2, and its productive aspects in Book 3. There are some excellent comments on the classification of rhetoric, showing Aristotle's influence, in Quintilian's great treatise, *The Education of the Orator* (2.18.2–5), leading to the conclusion that its primary role is that of a "practical" art.

D. ARISTOTLE'S ORIGINAL AUDIENCE AND HIS AUDIENCE TODAY

Since the publication of the first edition of this book there has been a resumption of the ongoing scholarly discussion about the audience for which *On Rhetoric* was composed and about how it should be read today.[26] In a prize-winning article entitled "Aristotle's *Rhetoric* Against Rhetoric: Unitarian Reading and Esoteric Hermeneutics," Carol Poster (1997) argued that Aristotle remained faithful to the ethical values of Plato's philosophical rhetoric and hostile to rhetoric as generally understood. In the aftermath of the execution of Socrates, however, he recognized that philosophers could be in danger. *On Rhetoric*, she concludes,

> is provided as a manual for the student trained in dialectic who needs, particularly for self-defense or defense of Platonic-Aristotelian philosophy, to sway an ignorant or corrupt audience or to understand the functioning of rhetoric within the badly ordered state. The techniques described are dangerous, potentially harmful to both the speaker and audience, and ought not be revealed to the general readership of Aristotle's dialogues, but only taught within the controlled environment of Aristotle's school, as part of the esoteric corpus of Platonic-Aristotelian teaching. (244)

A few years later, in "The Audience for Aristotle's *Rhetoric*," Edward W. Clayton (2004) examined the possible audiences Aristotle might have had in mind, including the legislator of an ideal city, the Athenian public or an elite subset of that public, the students in his philosophical school, or different audiences in different parts of the work, written at different times. He concludes that the students in his school are the most likely audience, agreeing in this with Poster, though without her emphasis on moral urgency.

The text of *On Rhetoric* that we read today is substantially the text left by Aristotle at his death and preserved in his personal library.[27] It was one of his "esoteric" works, not published and not available to readers generally until three hundred years later. Thus there is little doubt about the audience he envisioned for this text: students in his school in Athens in the years 335–323 B.C.E. It remains the case, however, that different parts of the text were originally composed at different times for a different audience, even if somewhat revised later. The part of the text most in question is what Rist (1989:84–85) called "the early core"—Book 1, chapters 5–15—though most parts of Book 3 are perhaps also early. By "early" is meant the 350s when Aristotle was a member of the Academy and is said to have given the "afternoon lectures" to a general audience.[28] Aristotle had earlier written and published the dialogue *Gryllus* in which he is said to have argued, perhaps with the school of Isocrates in mind, that rhetoric is not an "art" in the sense of a system or method. This is the position advanced by Socrates in Plato's *Gorgias*, but we know that Aristotle subsequently abandoned it, for in 1.1.2 he defines rhetoric as an art. Thus his ideas on rhetoric did develop from their Platonic base, perhaps in connection with teaching the subject for the first time, studying real speeches, and reading the handbooks, but he also never abandoned Plato's view of what rhetoric should be in an ideal society. He made a systematic collection of teachings from rhetorical handbooks, the *Synagōgē tekhnōn*, and though he criticizes these handbooks, in *Sophistical Refutations* he also acknowledges that progress had been made over time in constructing a systematic art of rhetoric. Poster's statement that Aristotle did not think the techniques of rhetoric should be revealed to a general readership is clearly an overstatement.

Aristotle's *Poetics* shows that he did not share Plato's moral scruples about poetry, but neither does he seem to regard it as a moral force. Indeed, unlike Plato and many later critics, Aristotle apparently did not believe that it was a function of poetry to provide ethical patterns of conduct, good or bad, for listeners or readers; at most, they might experience a beneficial and brief psychological catharsis of pity and fear. Much of his other research was devoted to physics and biology, and in these scientific works his ethical philosophy is temporarily set aside in the interests of discovering all that can be known. Aristotle, unlike Plato, was a formalist in the sense that he was interested in describing phenomena of the natural and social world on the basis of observation; he clearly became interested in rhetoric as a social phenomenon and potentially as a practical application of his theories of logic, and he was capable of giving a detached, objective account of it as of other subjects and of describing this to students.[29] This material he revised and inserted in *On Rhetoric* as we read it today, incorporating moral caveats against its improper use at the beginning of Books 1 and 3 and justifying study of it by philosophers on the basis of the corruption of contemporary society. It seems likely that Aristotle taught rhetoric to the young Alexander, and if so, what he would have taught him were practical skills in public speaking and an ability to evaluate speeches by others who came before him, with warnings about the moral dangers inherent in rhetoric.

Modern audiences for *On Rhetoric* fall roughly into four main groups, with considerable overlapping and many individual differences of opinion. One group consists of the classical philologists, specialists in Greek language, literature, and culture. Their special interest is textual and contextual, including comparisons of Aristotle's teaching with the practice of oratory, historiography, and other literature of his time and with political procedures in Athens, and it also includes efforts to date different parts of Aristotle's works on the basis of content, development of thought, and style. As a result of these studies, the philologists tend to pounce on inconsistencies in the text and thus resist viewing it as a unity.

A second group is that of the philosophers, largely scholars who study and teach ancient philosophy. They are naturally most interested in the philosophical content of *On Rhetoric* and in the relation of it to Aristotle's other philosophical works, as well as to the dialogues of Plato. Like their late-antique and medieval predecessors, they tend to approach Aristotelianism as a consistent whole, and they often defend the unity of *On Rhetoric* against the philologists. As skilled dialecticians, they are good at what they do and can easily overwhelm the average reader with their subtlety and learning, sometimes at the expense of distorting what Aristotle actually says.

The third group is that of teachers of English composition and speech communication, whose primary interest is in the rhetorical theory found in the work. They are understandably inclined to use it as the basis of developing a comprehensive system of rhetoric, following out the implications of the text or imaging what Aristotle ought to have said but didn't. They are especially interested in argumentation and in problems involving Aristotle's understanding of the enthymeme and its implications.

The fourth and smallest group is that of the literary scholars and critics. Their interest in the *Rhetoric* is largely confined to the third book, where Aristotle's theory of metaphor is of special interest, and they read the *Rhetoric* in conjunction with the *Poetics*.

E. THE STRENGTHS AND LIMITATIONS OF *ON RHETORIC*

The great strength of *On Rhetoric* derives from its clear recognition (in contrast to views expressed by Plato) that rhetoric is a technique or tool applicable to any subject and from the universality and utility of its basic, systematically organized, concepts. It provides a method for looking at rhetoric as a human phenomenon, for learning how to use it, and also for a system of criticism, in that the features of speech that Aristotle describes can be used not only to construct a speech, but also to analyze and evaluate other forms of discourse. The most important of the concepts that Aristotle uses as frameworks for his discussion are:

1. The identification of three (and only three) *pisteis*, or forms of persuasion, derived from the factors in any speech situation:
   a. Presentation of the trustworthy character of the speaker
   b. The logical argument set out in the text
   c. The emotional effect created by the speaker and text on the audience or reader
2. The distinction of three (and only three) species of rhetoric, based on whether the audience is or is not a *judge*, in the sense of being able to take specific action as a result of being persuaded to do so, and the *time* with which each species is concerned:
   a. If a judge of past actions, the species is *judicial*
   b. If a judge of future action, the species is *deliberative*
   c. If an observer of the speech, not called on to take action, the species is *epideictic*

   Each of these species has its characteristic "end," the principal issue with which it is concerned:
   a. The end of judicial rhetoric is justice
   b. The end of deliberative rhetoric is the best interest of the audience
   c. The end of epideictic rhetoric is praise or blame of the subject
3. Forms of persuasion are either:
   a. *Non-artistic*: direct evidence (facts, witnesses, documents, etc.) that the speaker uses but does not—or should not—invent; or
   b. *Artistic*: logical arguments constructed by the speaker, of two types:
      i. Inductive argument, called paradigm, or example, drawing a particular conclusion from one or more parallels

ii. Deductive argument, called enthymeme, or rhetorical syllogism, drawing a conclusion from stated or implied premises

4. In rhetoric the speaker or writer almost always deals with probabilities—what could have happened or can happen based on what happens for the most part in such situations.
5. The materials of enthymemes come from the premises of other disciplines, especially politics and ethics, but their formal structure draws on *topics*, strategies of argument useful in dealing with any subject.

On Rhetoric is strong in its emphasis on the importance of logical validity. There are also valuable concepts in the discussion of style, especially the demand for clarity, the understanding of the effect of different kinds of language and sentence structure, and the explication of the role of metaphor. The work is also of interest in that it summarizes many of the political and moral assumptions of contemporary Greek society and preserves many quotations from writers or speakers that we would not otherwise have.

As in all of his philosophy, in describing rhetoric Aristotle sought to discover what was universally true, and to a considerable extent he was successful. His system of rhetoric can, and has been, used to describe the phenomenon of speech in cultures as diverse from the Greeks as the ancient Hebrews, the Chinese, and primitive societies around the world; and it can be used to describe many features of modern communication.

The treatise nevertheless has limitations and needs to be expanded or revised to provide a complete, general rhetoric. With only occasional exceptions, its focus is on public address or civic discourse and is somewhat conditioned by the circumstances and conventions of the forms with which he was familiar. Epideictic discourse, in particular, needs to be looked at in a variety of ways not recognized by Aristotle. He thought of it as the rhetoric of praise or blame, as in a funeral oration or a denunciation of someone, and failed to formulate its role in the instilling, preservation, or enhancement of cultural values, even though this was clearly a major function, as seen in Pericles' famous *Funeral Oration* or the epideictic speeches of Isocrates. His apparent lack of interest in the moral value of epideictic rhetoric is perhaps influenced by scorn for Isocrates, but it is also analogous to his feelings about poetry mentioned earlier.

Aristotle's theory of *ēthos* is striking, but he limits it to the effect of character as conveyed by the words of a speaker and he fails to recognize the great role of the authority of a speaker as already perceived by an audience.[30] He limits non-artistic means of persuasion to direct evidence that can be used in a trial, while the concept should perhaps be enlarged to include the appearance and authority of a speaker, features of the setting and the context of a speech that affect its reception, and other factors that a speaker can use for persuasive ends.

Another problem with the work is Aristotle's failure to illustrate and relate to rhetoric many of the political and ethical topics he discusses. Chapters 4 and 5 of Book 1, for example, give no suggestions about how to use political topics in a speech, and chapters 6–14 could have benefited from showing more clearly how this material can be employed. Similarly, the description of the emotions in Book 2, chapters 2–11, fails to draw examples from the rhetorical situation. Aristotle probably had a rather limited knowledge of Greek political oratory; in addition to epideictic orations, which he quotes, some deliberative and judicial orations were available in published form, but he seems to have made no effort to construct his theory of rhetoric by analysis of real speeches.[31] Instead, he relies on constructing arguments based on his understanding of the goals of politics and ethics. Great emphasis is put on understanding the enthymeme as the key to logical persuasion, but its theoretical importance is probably exaggerated, since its syllogistic qualities are very slippery, and Aristotle's precepts can be reduced to a recommendation that a speaker give a reason (or apparent reason) for what is asserted. Although he mentions different kinds of questions that may be at issue in a trial—questions of fact or definition of the law, for example—he fails to give adequate priority to a method for determining these questions in planning a speech, something which was later supplied by the development of stasis theory.[32] Some problems with the work result from different parts having been written at different times, and though there are signs of revisions and addition of cross-references, Aristotle never completed the process, leaving not only precepts unapplied to public address, but also inconsistencies both in doctrine and in terminology—for example, his varying uses of *pistis* and *topos*. Nor does Aristotle take a strong stand against the common Greek preference for circumstantial evidence over the direct evidence of documents and witnesses.

F. CHAPTER-BY-CHAPTER OUTLINE OF *ON RHETORIC*

To clarify the overall structure of *On Rhetoric* and to give readers an initial understanding of its coverage, a chapter-by-chapter outline of the work follows. The book divisions originated with Aristotle and represent convenient lengths for a papyrus scroll in Aristotle's time.

The chapter divisions were first made by George of Trebizond in the fifteenth century and in most cases represent logical units.

Books 1–2: *Pisteis*, or The Means of Persuasion in Public Address

Book 1: Introduction; Definition and Divisions of the Subject to be Discussed; Special Topics Useful in Deliberative, Epideictic, and Judicial Rhetoric

Chapters 1–3: Introductory

Chapter 1: Introduction to Rhetoric for Students of Dialectic
2: Definition of Rhetoric; Means of Persuasion; Topics
3: The Three Species of Rhetoric: Deliberative, Judicial, Epideictic

Chapters 4–15: *Idia*, or Specific Topics in Each of the Three Species

Chapters 4–8: Topics for Deliberative Rhetoric

Chapter 4: Political Topics
5: Ethical Topics
6: Ethical Topics Continued: Definition of a "Good"
7: The "Common" Topic of Degree of Magnitude
8: Topics About Constitutions

Chapter 9: Topics for Epideictic Rhetoric; Amplification

Chapters 10–15: Topics for Judicial Rhetoric

Chapter 10: Topics About Wrongdoing
11: Topics About Pleasure
12: Topics About Wrongdoers and Those Wronged
13: Topics About Justice and Injustice
14: The "Common" Topic of Degree of Magnitude in Judicial Rhetoric
15: Non-artistic Means of Persuasion: Laws, Witnesses, Contracts, Tortures, Oaths

Book 2: *Pisteis*, or The Means of Persuasion, Continued

Chapter 1: Introduction; Character and the Emotions as Means of Persuasion

Chapters 2–11: Propositions About the Emotions

Chapter 2: Anger
3: Calmness
4: Friendly Feeling and Enmity
5: Fear and Confidence

6: Shame and Shamelessness
7: Kindliness and Unkindliness
8–9: Pity and Indignation
10–11: Envy and Emulation

Chapters 12–17: Adapting the Character of a Speaker to the Character of the Audience

Chapter 12: Character of the Young
13: Character of the Old
14: Character of Those in the Prime of Life
15: Character of the Wellborn
16: Character of the Wealthy
17: Character of the Powerful

Chapters 18–26: Forms of Logical Argument

Chapter 18: Introduction
19: Topics "Common" to All Species of Rhetoric
20: Argument from Example (Paradigm)
21: Maxims in Arguments
22: Enthymemes
23: Twenty-eight Common Topics, or Lines of Argument
24: Fallacious Enthymemes
25: Refutation of Enthymemes
26: Amplification, Refutation, and Objection

Book 3: Delivery, Style, and Arrangement

Chapters 1–12: Prose Style

Chapter 1: Summary of Books 1–2; Remarks on Delivery; Origins of Artistic Prose
2: The Virtue of Style
3: Faults in Diction
4: Similes
5: Grammatical Correctness
6: Expansiveness in Composition
7: Appropriateness
8: Prose Rhythm
9: Periodic Style
10: Urbanities and Visualization
11: Metaphor and Other Devices of Style
12: Oral and Written Styles

Chapters 13–19: Arrangement

Chapter 13: The Necessary Parts of a Speech
14: The Prooemion
15: Ways of Meeting a Prejudicial Attack

16: The Narration
17: The Proof
18: Interrogation
19: The Epilogue

Notes

1. For further information, see Düring 1957 and Rist 1989.

2. For information on the Academy and life there, see *Brill's New Pauly: Encyclopaedia of the Ancient World*, vol. 1, coll. 41–42.

3. See especially Aristotle's discussion in *Nicomachean Ethics* 1.6 and in *Metaphysics* 1.6.

4. A seminal work was that of Jaeger (1934), which argued for initial acceptance of Platonic doctrines and a growing independence of thought over time; for criticism and more recent views, see Wians 1996.

5. The most famous passage in which Socrates (i.e., Plato) criticizes writing comes at the end of Plato's *Phaedrus*.

6. Discussion by Chroust 1965.

7. See Lossau 1974.

8. The sources are Cicero, *On the Orator* 3.141, *Tusculan Disputations* 1.4.7, and *Orator* 46; Philodemus, *On Rhetoric* 2.50–51 ed. Sudhaus; Quintilian 3.1.14; Diogenes Laertius 5.3; Syrianus 2.5 ed. Rabe. Philodemus severely blames Aristotle for abandoning philosophy to teach rhetoric; see Chroust 1964.

9. See Rist 1989:136–144.

10. Isocrates, *Epistle* 5. He says that Alexander "does not even reject eristic" and regards it as a valuable private exercise but realizes it is unsuitable for a ruler to allow anyone to contradict him.

11. Plato names Isocrates only once, in an enigmatic passage at the end of *Phaedrus*. Aristotle quotes or refers to Isocrates some thirty-nine times in the *Rhetoric*, but rarely elsewhere.

12. See Lynch 1972.

13. It used to be thought that Corax and Tisias were two different people, but it is likely that Corax was a nickname for Tisias; see Cole 1991b and Appendix II.A.

14. Cf., e.g., Plato, *Gorgias* 449c.

15. According to Philostratus, *Lives of the Sophists* 1.9.11, Gorgias was the first to do this. Types of sophistic discourse can be seen in Socrates' encounters with sophists; see especially *Protagoras* 320c.

16. The speeches in Plato's *Symposium* are also sophistic in style, but not ostensibly intended to teach rhetorical technique.

17. We do not know whether the speech in the text was actually a work by Lysias or, more likely, a deliberately bad imitation by Plato.

18. See Radermacher 1951:B X 13–15; B XVII 1; B XVIII 1.

19. This word will recur from time to time in later passages. "Eristic" is a derivative of *eris*, "strife," and refers to argument for the sake of argument with little recourse to sound logic.

20. "Tisias after the first." Whom Aristotle regarded as "the first" is uncertain. One possibility is Empedocles (Diogenes Laertius 7.57–58; Quintilian 3.1.8). "The first" probably did not refer to Corax; see Appendix II.A.

21. For a translation of this unusual work, see Sprague 1972:42–46.

22. Dionysius of Halicarnassus says (*On Composition of Words* 12; p. 84) that Gorgias tried to define *kairos*, what was timely said, but did not write anything worth mentioning about it. Perhaps he just gave examples of timely statements.

23. See, e.g., Cicero, *On the Orator* 3.141.

24. See Isocrates' remarks in *Against the Sophists* and the *Letter to Alexander*.

25. See Cicero, *On Invention* 2.8; Solmsen 1941.

26. An earlier discussion was that of Lord 1981.

27. In a paper at the 2005 convention of the National Communication Association, Brad McAdon argued that the text we call *On Rhetoric* is a compilation of material by Aristotle, Theophrastus, and others, which was made in the first century B.C.E. by Andronicus. This is an extension of views found in McAdon 2001 and 2004 and is, at most, probably exaggerated; see further, Appendix II.B.

28. For the sources, see above, Introduction A, n. 8.

29. Cf. Hill 1981.

30. This probably results from the fact that speakers in the law courts and political assemblies were often not well-known individuals. What counted was not who they were but what they said.

31. See Trevett 1996.

32. Cf. Liu 1991.

Section Five: The Design of Expression: Figures of Speech, Tropes, and Rhetorical Devices

Section Five

The Design of Expression: Figures of Speech, Tropes and Rhetorical Devices

The greatest thing by far is to be a master of metaphor—Aristotle

Shall I compare you to a summer's day?
Thou art more lovely and more temperate
Rough winds do shake the darling buds of May,
And summer's lease hath all too short a date
Sometime too hot the eye of heaven shines . . .
But thy eternal summer shall not fade . . . —Shakespeare

Well there's a light in your eye that keeps shining
Like a star that can't wait for the night
I hate to think I've been blinded baby—Led Zeppelin

As we have seen and as we will continue to see, rhetoric is fundamentally concerned with effective and persuasive communication. This powerful type of communication comes in many forms with many strategies that influences our sense of logic, provokes our passions and appeals to our ethics. Yet, in application, what makes rhetoric so powerful? Wherein lays the effectiveness? It is with figurative language that the nature of communication becomes transcendent. The metaphor leans over the motionless body of letters and words and breathes life into what was once inanimate. So it is with this in mind that we turn our attention to figures of speech, tropes and rhetorical devices.

Aristotle devotes the third section of *On Rhetoric*, to Delivery, Style and Arrangement and the Origins of Artistic Prose. In this section Aristotle addresses aspects of language use and word choice. Among many particulars he analyzes issues of appropriateness, grammaticality, rhythm, metaphor and the virtues of style. The result of understanding the use of these speech attributes is to create communication that is more vivid.

We will see in subsequent chapters the significance of the four faculties of the mind as stated by David Hume and elaborated upon by George Campbell. But for now we will concentrate on the Faculty of Imagination. The imagination houses the mental power of producing and recombining images and concepts in order to create new modes of expression. The imagination is the place of conception for figurative language. It is the deep resourcefulness of the imagination that allows us to produce a mental "image." The image is then the essence of artistic language. The image is the distinctive element of art, written or otherwise, by which experience in all its richness and complexity is communicated. Thus as rhetoricians, we must be aware of the design of expression if we seek to communicate effectively, persuasively and profoundly.

Open the day and see it be the window.
—*The Garden of Eloquence*, Henry Peacham

We will understand figures of speech to be a form of speech artfully varied from common usage. Figures of speech are various uses of language that depart from customary construction, order, meaning or significance. It is language in which meaning is not literal but figurative. Figurative language often equates to representational and symbolic expressions. Figures of speech can be divided into two main groups: schemes and tropes. A scheme is a departure from the ordinary pattern or arrangement of words. A trope is any literary or rhetorical device that uses words in other than their literal sense. Both tropes and schemes involve a transference of meaning because the literal sense of a word or sequence is changed to achieve new communication expectations. The following are some examples:

- Metaphor—an analogy identifying one object with another and ascribing to the first object qualities of the second object; an implied comparison between two things of unlike nature that yet have something in common; the word is used not in its literal sense, but in one analogous to it. A metaphor functions with a tenor and vehicle. The tenor is notion or **idea** being expressed. The vehicle is the **image** by which the idea is conveyed.

Life's but a walking shadow; a poor player,
That struts and frets his hour upon the stage.—Shakespeare

Life is a beach.

Love is a temple
You ask me to enter
But then you make me crawl.—U2

- Simile—a similarity between two objects or concepts that is directly expressed using the words "like" or "as."

You are like a hurricane: there's calm in your eye, but I'm getting blown away—
Neil Young

Let us go then, you and I,
While the evening is spread out against the sky,
Like a patient etherized upon a table . . . —T. S. Eliot

Words are flowing out like
Endless rain into a paper cup
They slither while they pass
They slip away across the universe.—The Beatles

- Allegory—a form of an extended or elaborate metaphor in which objects, persons, and actions in a narrative are equated with meanings that lie outside of the narrative itself; symbolic use of language that is sustained throughout a literary work.

  "The Road Not Taken"—Robert Frost

  The Wall—Pink Floyd

  These works taken in their entirety can be considered allegorical works.

- Personification—the assignment of human traits or abilities to something non-human or inanimate; attribution of personality behaviors to an impersonal thing.

  In the dark pines the wind disentangles itself . . .
  Days, all one kind, go chasing each other.—Pablo Neruda

  While my guitar gently weeps . . . —The Beatles

- Hyperbole—an intentional exaggeration used to amplify meaning or emphasize a certain effect.

  Here once the embattled farmers stood
  And fired the shot heard round the world.
  —Ralph Waldo Emerson, "Concord Hymn"

  And quiet is the thought of you, the file on you complete,
  Except what we forgot to do, a thousand kisses deep.—Leonard Cohen

- Metonymy—the substitution of the name of something with a word that it is closely associated with; usually a single word connected to a large idea or framework; a contiguity of words and images such as "crown" for monarchy, "the cloth" for priesthood and "White House" for presidency.

- Alliteration—the repetition of the same sound beginning several words in sequence; it is most often the repetition of initial consonants.

  Let us go forth to lead the land we love.—John F. Kennedy

Voilà! In view, a humble vaudevillian veteran, cast vicariously as both victim and villain by the vicissitudes of Fate. This visage, no mere veneer of vanity, is a vestige of the vox populi, now vacant, vanished. However, this valorous visitation of a bygone vexation, stands vivified and has vowed to vanquish these venal and virulent vermin vanguarding vice and the violently vicious and voracious violation of volition.—V from *V for Vendetta*

- Litotes and Meiosis—the deliberate use of understatement as a means of enhancement by denying the contrary of the thing being affirmed.

"It's just a flesh wound."—said by a knight being dismembered as absurd humor in *Monty Python and the Holy Grail*

"I'm really glad that you have come to visit," said the spider to the fly.

- Oxymoron—the placing of two ordinarily opposing terms adjacent to one another creating a compressed paradox; the use of two terms that are customarily contradictory as in such phrases as "bitter sweet" and "jumbo shrimp."

I must be cruel only to be kind.—Shakespeare

The sounds of silence—Simon and Garfunkel

- Irony—a broad term touching upon a variety of rhetoric devices referring to the recognition of a reality different from appearance; the expression of something which is contrary to the intended meaning; the words say one thing but mean another.

  There are different kinds of irony.

  Tragic (or dramatic) irony occurs when a character on stage or in a story is ignorant, but the audience watching knows his or her eventual fate.

  Socratic irony takes place when someone (classically a teacher) pretends to be foolish or ignorant, to expose the ignorance of another.

  Cosmic irony is when a higher being or force interferes in a character's life, creating ironic settings.

- Anaphora and Epistrophe—one of the devices of repetition; the repetition of a word or phrase at the beginning or end of successive phrases, clauses or lines; the repetition of words establishes a rhythm that can produce strong themes.

I celebrate myself and sing myself
And what I assume you shall assume,
For every atom belonging to me as good belongs to you.
—Walt Whitman, *Song of Myself*

This is radio clash on pirate satellite.
This is radio clash using audio ammunition
This is radio clash can we get that world to listen.—The Clash

... here is the root of the root and the bud of the bud
and the sky of the sky of a tree called life ... —e. e. cummings

- Paradox—an assertion seemingly opposed to common sense, but that may yet have some truth in it.

Art is a form of lying in order to tell the truth.—Pablo Picasso

What a pity that youth must be wasted on the young.
—George Bernard Shaw

The preceding list reveals some of the more significant figures of speech, but realize that there are many more. There are numerous tropes and schemes that explain the particulars, detailed nuances and subtle distinctions within stylized language use. As a student of rhetoric you should be aware of the different types of figures of speech and employ them judiciously and thoughtfully in your rhetorical behavior. It is with these methods that the speaker moves the listener and the writer influences the reader. It is in this manner that the potential of rhetoric, thus the potential of significant communication is realized.

These themes are best summed up by John Quincy Adams, the sixth President of the United States and previously the first Boylston Professor of Rhetoric at Harvard University. Adams concluded his Inaugural Oration with this challenge: *"Gather fragrance from the whole paradise of science and learn to distill from your lips all the honey of persuasion. Consecrate above all, the faculties of your life to the cause of truth, of freedom and of humanity. So shall your country ever gladden at the sound of your voice and every talent added to your accomplishments, become another blessing to mankind."*

It is with this in mind that we continue to study rhetoric and uncover the significance of its interpersonal and social promise.

Bibliography

Burton, Gideon. "Silva Rhetoricae." Brigham Young University. February 2007. http://humanities.byu.edu/rhetoric/silva.htm.

Connors, Robert J. and Edward P. J. Corbett. *Classical Rhetoric for the Modern Student.* New York, Oxford: Oxford University Press, 1999.

Harmon, William and C. Hugh Holman. *A Handbook to Literature.* New York: Macmillan Publishing Company, 1992.

Scaife, Ross. "A Glossary of Rhetorical Terms." Department of Modern & Classical Languages, Literatures, & Cultures, University of Kentucky, December 2004. http://www.uky.edu/AS/Classics/rhetoric.html#related.

Section Six: The Belletristic Movement

Section Six
The Belletristic Movement

Timothy Borchers

At this point in our study, two significant paths emerge in Western rhetoric. On one path, which we will study in the remaining part of this chapter, rhetorical scholars continued to be interested in the style and delivery of rhetoric. Specifically, we'll examine how the belletristic and elocutionary movements in Great Britain furthered the emphasis on style and delivery that had characterized the study of rhetoric since the end of the Roman Empire. At the same time, however, another group of scholars in Great Britain and Europe began studying science, in general, and psychology, in particular, in a systematic, scientific manner. These scholars are often known as the epistemologists. Given the close relationship between psychology and rhetoric, they naturally addressed issues of rhetoric in their study and teaching. Since this type of study is quite different than that of the belletristic and elocutionary movements, we'll study the work of the epistemologists in the next chapter. Refer back to Table 3.1 to see the relationship between the various schools of thought concerning rhetoric during this time period. The work of the epistemologists evolved into a study of argumentation, which we will also take up in the next chapter. For now, let us return to the belletristic movement.

The **belletristic movement** significantly expanded the scope of rhetoric, but maintained the focus on style and delivery. Instead of viewing rhetoric as public speaking, or even sermon making, belletristic rhetoricians also focused on stylistic elements of belles letters, or literature and art. *Belles lettres,* from which the word *belletristic* is derived, literally means "beautiful letters."

Golden and Corbett (1968) defined this movement as follows:

> This approach was based on the concept that rhetoric and related polite arts, poetry, drama, art, history, biography, philology, and so on should be joined under the broad heading of rhetoric and belles letters. Since these disciplines share a common interest in taste, style, criticism, and sublimity, they seek to instruct the student to become an effective practitioner and judge in written and oral communication. (p. 8)

Ferreira-Buckley (1994) explained that belletristic rhetoricians "studied matters now encompassed under such diverse subjects as criticism, grammar, hermeneutics, linguistics, logic, poetics, psychology, rhetoric, and semiotics" (p. 23). The belletristic movement was influenced by Aristotle's *Poetics,* Isocrates' *Antidosis,* Longinus's *On the Sublime,* and Horace's *Ars Poetica.* Thus, these scholars sought to revive classical works concerning style.

BOX 3.4 Biography of a Theorist: Hugh Blair

Hugh Blair, one of the great theorists of the belletristic movement, was born on April 7, 1718 in Edinburgh, Scotland. He studied the humanities, Greek, logic, and natural philosophy at the University of Edinburgh. He received a master's degree in 1739, and his study included rhetoric. In October 1741, Blair was licensed to preach by the Presbytery of Edinburgh. He was ordained in 1743 and elected to preach at the Canongate Church. He preached there for eleven years. During this time, Blair studied Shakespeare and the sermons of Frederick Carmichael. He would later preach at Lady Yester's Church and the High Church of St. Giles, the most influential church in Edinburgh. He began conducting lectures on rhetoric. His teaching was so popular that King George III created the Regius Professorship for him; Blair served in that capacity until he retired in 1783. He immediately published his lectures, *Lectures on Rhetoric and Belles Lettres*. Blair died in 1800 and is buried near Greyfriars Church in Edinburgh.

Harding (1965) noted that *Lectures of Rhetoric and Belles Lettres* was "the kind of book Quintilian produced for the first century A.D. Blair selected and restated the teachings of writers like Aristotle, Longinus, Cicero, and Quintilian. He then exemplified their theories by the use of passages from English writers" (Harding, 1965, p. vii). The lectures in this book were printed nearly without revision from when he presented them, in some cases twenty years previously. The book contains forty-seven lectures, which were created for a college-age audience. Keep in mind that during this period, college students were often younger than they are today, some as young as thirteen or fourteen. Harding summarizes Blair's contribution to the study of rhetoric: "It is still certain that he did more to interpret and make known the rhetorical theory of the ancients than any other British or American rhetorical writer" (p. vii).

The belletristic movement is also credited with developing the practice of rhetorical criticism. Although rhetorical theorists as far back as Aristotle and the Sophists were interested in critiquing rhetorical practice, their focus was clearly on how rhetors could learn the rhetorical principles necessary to give an effective speech. Thus, rhetorical theory—in our previous study—was interested in generating effective rhetorical practice. Belletristic scholars began to use rhetorical theory in a different way, to analyze and critique rhetorical practice for its own sake. Ferreira-Buckley (1994) notes, "As rhetoric's analytic function became more prominent—eventually obscuring its generative function—rhetoric became literary theory" (p. 23). Thus, belletristic scholars used rhetoric to analyze and critique such diverse forms as Shakespeare's plays, sermons, and poetry instead of viewing rhetorical theory as a way to develop effective communication. If you recall our discussion in the previous chapter and that of St. Augustine in this chapter, the goal for many of the theorists was to develop a theory that would lead to effective rhetorical practice. This goal became less important for subsequent theorists.

Adam Smith and Hugh Blair are often credited with being the most influential belletristic scholars. Smith, most acclaimed for his economic work, *The Wealth of Nations,* was a Scottish professor who also delivered a series of lectures on rhetoric. Not generally noted for his rhetorical ability, Smith never achieved the prominence of Blair. An audience member of Smith's, Blair would later gain much more publicity and royal support for his rhetorical teaching. Generally, regarded as the most significant of the belletristic scholars, we'll look at Blair's work in greater detail here. First, though, read more about Blair in Box 3.4, Biography of a Theorist.

Since Blair's work is most representative of the belletristic movement (Warnick, 1993), we'll study his ideas in more depth here. Blair's lectures concerning rhetoric and belles letters were published after his retirement in 1783. The publishing company, by the way, paid him 1,500 pounds for the lectures, making him the highest paid author on rhetoric to date (Ferreira-Buckley 1994, p. 24). His book, *Lectures on Rhetoric and Belles Lettres,* was made up of two volumes of over one thousand pages. It contained forty-seven separate lectures, including an introductory lecture, four lectures on taste, four on language, fifteen on style, ten on eloquence, and thirteen on criticism. Potter (1965) noted that for students of rhetoric, twenty-seven lectures hold the most importance. Let's examine Blair's ideas about rhetoric contained in this seminal work. For a summary of the forty-seven lectures contained in this book, consult the website http://www.msu.edu/user/ransford/summaries.html.

Taste

Taste, explained Blair (1965), is "the power of receiving pleasure from the beauties of nature and of art" (p. 16). All people, said Blair, have some sense of taste. He explained, "Nothing that belongs to human nature is more universal than the relish of beauty of one kind of another; of what is orderly, proportioned, grand, harmonious, new, or sprightly" (p. 17). Despite its universal nature, not all people perceive taste in the same way. There are great inequalities in what people consider to be beautiful. Yet Blair believed that taste could be improved with education. He explained, "Taste is a most improvable faculty, if there be any such in human nature" (p. 19). Yet he also observed that there is no one standard of taste for every situation. At the same time, taste is "far from being an arbitrary principle" (p. 34).

The two primary characteristics of taste are delicacy and correctness, according to Blair. Delicacy refers to the ability to see things in beauty that others may not see. Blair explained that one who has a sense of delicacy "sees distinctions and differences where others see none; the most latent beauty does not escape him, and he is sensible of the smallest blemish" (1965, p. 24). Correctness refers to consistently using the proper standard when evaluating items of beauty. Blair explained, "A man of correct Taste is one who is never imposed on by counterfeit beauties; who carries always in his mind that standard of good sense which he employs in judging every thing" (p. 24). Delicacy is an innate trait, while correctness can be learned.

There are several sources of pleasure, according to Blair. The first is grandeur, or sublimity. Blair saw these terms as synonymous. Though everyone has a conception of these terms, Blair wrote that "it is not easy to describe, in words, the precise impression which great and sublime objects make upon us, when we behold them" (1965, p. 46). The emotion associated with grandeur and sublimity is delightful, but serious with degrees of "awfulness" and "solemnity." Beautiful objects, by comparison, produce a more "gay" or "brisk" emotion. Nature, with its extended plains or boundless oceans, provides examples of grandeur and sublimity. A tall mountain, Blair wrote, is even more grand or sublime than the ocean.

Likewise, thunder or the roaring of wind can be sublime because of its sound. In short, "mighty power and strength" account for the sublime.

Writing or speech that references mighty and forceful objects and that affects the imagination achieves sublimity. Blair's view of the sublime differs in some ways from Longinus's view. For Blair, sublime rhetoric must discuss a sublime object. Further, the object must be presented "in such a light as is most proper to give us a clear and full impression of it; it must be described with strength, with conciseness, and simplicity" (1965, p. 60). The rhetor, or poet, must be "deeply affected, and warmed, by" the sublime idea being expressed. Blair noted, "If his own feeling be languid, he can never inspire us with any strong emotion" (p. 60). In particular, the scriptures provide "the highest instances of the Sublime" (p. 61).

Another source of pleasure is beauty. "Beauty, next to Sublimity, affords, beyond doubt, the highest pleasure to the imagination," noted Blair (1965, p. 80). Beauty raises a calmer, more gentle emotion than the sublime. Although sublimity is not lasting, the emotions caused by beauty are of "longer continuance" (p. 81). Color, shape, curves, and motion are all qualities of beauty. In rhetoric, beauty can be achieved by writing or speaking with a certain grace that "neither lifts the mind very high, nor agitates it very much, but diffuses over the imagination an agreeable and pleasing serenity" (p. 90).

Several additional sources of pleasure can be briefly summarized:

- Novelty is noticed by the audience and creates an agreeable emotion.
- Imitation pleases because it reminds us of the original object or idea.
- Melody and harmony, either poetically or musically, delight audience members.

Language

Blair, following his discussion of taste, turned to language. The four lectures on language serve as a precursor to the more lengthy treatment of style. In fact, Blair explained that language "is the foundation of the whole power of eloquence" (1965, p. 97). Blair defined language as the "expression of our ideas by certain articulate sounds, which are used as the signs of those ideas" (p. 98). Language can be used to communicate "the most delicate and refined emotions" of a person's mind to another. In the four chapters in which Blair discusses language, he focuses on the origin and development of language, the structure, or grammar, of language, and, specifically, the English language.

Style

Language is the means through which a person expresses style, noted Blair. He defined style as "the peculiar manner in which a man expresses his conceptions, by means of Language" (1965, p. 183). Blair offers a particularly vivid illustration of this definition by saying style "is a picture of the ideas which rise" in the mind of the speaker. The style of a rhetor cannot readily be separated from his or her sentiments. Language is but the means through which those sentiments are expressed, in either written or oral form.

Blair explained that style has two qualities: perspicuity and ornament. He explained,

> For all that can possibly be required of Language, is, to convey our ideas clearly to the minds of others, and, at the same time, in such a dress, as by pleasing and interesting them, shall most effectively strengthen the impressions which we seek to make. When both these ends are answered, we certainly accomplish every purpose for which we use Writing and Discourse. (p. 184)

Perspicuity, Blair elaborated, is using language in a way that clearly states the speaker's ideas. He said that rhetoric must be obvious even to negligent listeners and strike them as the light of the sun on their eyes even when they are not looking upwards. He explained, "Perspicuity in writing, is not to be considered as only a sort of negative virtue, or freedom from defect. It has higher merit: It is a degree of positive beauty. We are pleased with an author, we consider him as deserving praise, who frees us from all fatigue of searching for his meaning" (p. 186).

Perspicuity has three qualities: purity, propriety, and precision. Purity refers to using words that are "of the language which we speak" and not "imported from other Languages" (Blair, 1965, p. 187). We might consider this today to mean that a rhetor is to use words that are commonly understood, not exotic words or slang words which do not have designated meanings. Propriety means to use the right word. A rhetor's words should be "correct" and "significant." Propriety, then, refers to the specific words chosen by the rhetor to communicate a specific idea. Precision avoids superfluous words and expressions and gets to the point of the speaker's idea. Blair noted that to "write with precision" one must have "distinctness and accuracy in his manner of thinking" (p. 189). A speaker should avoid saying more than he or she intends to have precision. Blair spends a great deal of time distinguishing between the meanings of words, so as to achieve propriety, and later on how to construct precise sentences.

Read the following passage from Federal Reserve Board Chair Alan Greenspan and consider how he achieved purity, propriety, and precision:

> Partly as a result of the balance-sheet restructuring, business credit quality appears to have recuperated considerably over the past few years. Last year, the default rate on bonds fell sharply, recovery rates on defaulted issues rose, the number of rating downgrades moderated substantially, and delinquencies on business loans continued to decline. The improved balance sheets and strong profits of business firms, together with attractive terms for financing in open markets and from banks, suggest that financial conditions remain quite supportive of further gains in capital spending in coming quarters. (February 11, 2004)

In this passage, Greenspan met each of Blair's standards of perspicuity:

- Despite the highly technical nature of Greenspan's testimony and his position as expert on global economics, Greenspan's speech is not filled with unfamiliar terminology. Although it may require some background in economics to make sense of a few key terms, Greenspan's speech largely has purity.
- In particular, Greenspan's speech reflected the quality of propriety. That is, Greenspan chose very specific words for his ideas. Since the wording he uses in his testimony to Congress influences international economic markets, Greenspan must be careful of his word choice.
- The link between Greenspan's economic mind and his rhetoric is clearly evident in the precision of his language. Greenspan's remarks say no more or less than he intends to say, and he clearly identifies limits and opportunities for the U.S. economy without embellishing or shading his meanings.

A second element of style is ornament. We have previously said that ornament concerns how words are pleasing and interesting for the listener. Ornament is achieved through graceful, strong, or melodious sentences or by figurative language. A graceful sentence has unity, which means that "There must always be some connecting principles among the parts" (Blair, 1965, p. 216). That is, a sentence should discuss one idea, should have a consistent tense and voice, and should be a complete unit of thought. A strong sentence, according to Blair, includes using capital letters for words at places that would make the fullest impression, arranging sentences so that the ideas became stronger from sentence to sentence, and avoiding concluding a sentence with an adverb, preposition, or inconsiderable word. Melodious sentences use pauses—in the form of commas or periods—effectively and they have an imaginative cadence.

The second aspect of ornament is figurative language. We have discussed figures of speech and figures of thought previously— in Chapter 2 and earlier in this chapter, in connection with Longinus. According to Blair, the use of figures enriches language and bestows dignity upon the style of the speaker or writer. Figurative language is also more pleasing for the listener and provides a more striking view of the object being discussed. Blair spent an entire lecture on metaphor, another topic we have discussed previously. The effect of a metaphor, wrote Blair "is to give light and strength to description; to make intellectual ideas, in some sort, visible to the eye, by giving them color, and substance, and sensible qualities" (1965, p. 297). Metaphors should be used "with a delicate hand" to avoid "confusion" and "inaccuracy" (p. 297). Blair then provided several rules for using metaphors effectively. He also discussed several specific figures, including apostrophe, personification, and allegory.

Blair concluded his lectures on style by focusing on different types of style and ways of creating effective style. Some of the rules Blair provided for creating an effective style include:

- Rhetors should have knowledge about the subject of which they are writing or speaking. Blair explained, "The foundation of all good Style, is good sense accompanied with a lively imagination" (p. 402). Blair here reiterated a point made earlier, that to have an effective style, one must have clear thoughts about the subject.

- Rhetors should expose themselves to the best writers and speakers. Blair wrote, "This is requisite, both in order to form a just taste in Style, and to supply us with a full stock of words on every subject" (p. 405). Students of style should not simply imitate the style of the great authors, though.
- Rhetors should adapt their style to the situation and audience. He noted, "Nothing merits the name of eloquent or beautiful, which is not suited to the occasion, and to the persons to whom it is addressed." (p. 406)

Blair's final lecture on style is a criticism of the style used in one of the publications of that time. By focusing on a particular example, Blair sought to illustrate what he had discussed concerning style, to observe any characteristics of style he may not have discussed, and to show the practicality of the subject matter.

Eloquence

Rhetoric, as defined by Blair, comprised a great variety of subjects, including drama, literature, and poetry. Thus, much of what he discussed concerning style focused mostly on written forms of rhetoric. In the twenty-fifth lecture, Blair turns his attention specifically to eloquence, or public speaking. Here, his focus is mostly on delivery of the spoken word. Blair, though, clearly saw style as relating to public speaking. His discussion of public speaking assumes that the speaker has knowledge of style and taste. He defines eloquence as "the Art of Speaking in such a manner as to attain the end for which we speak. Whenever a man speaks or writes, he is supposed, as a rational being, to have some end in view; either to inform, or to amuse, or to persuade, or, in some way or other, to act upon his fellow-creatures. He who speaks, or writes, in such a manner as to adapt all his words most effectually to that end, is the most eloquent man" (Blair, 1965, p. 2).

Blair identified the purpose of speaking as threefold: to inform, to persuade, and to amuse. Of these, he saw persuasion as the "most important subject of discourse" (p. 2). Consequently, Blair defined eloquence as "The Art of Persuasion" (p. 3). Blair distinguished between convincing and persuading, saying that conviction "affects the understanding only; persuasion, the will and the practice" (p. 3). Thus, persuasion involves the listener taking action on what is said. Convincing is possible based on "mere" reason and argument, but to persuade, the speaker must have passion. Noting that persuasion also requires freedom on the part of the listeners to follow what is said, Blair provided a brief history of rhetoric, from the days of the Greek Republic to the Roman Republic to the "modern times" of eighteenth century Great Britain. Blair noted, "Here, it must be confessed, that, in no European nation, Public Speaking has been considered as so great an object, or been cultivated with so much care, as in Greece and Rome" (p. 37). Blair observed that in all areas of British speaking, from the Parliament to the courts to the pulpit, public speaking did not enjoy the popularity or significance that it did in the ancient Greek and Roman Republics.

The most effective persuasive speaker had a "solid argument, clear method, a character of probity appearing in the Speaker, joined with such graces of Style and utterance, as shall draw our attention to what he says" (Blair, 1965, p. 3). Persuasion begins with good sense and solid argument. Blair also said that "proper method" was important, meaning that everything "should be found in its proper place" (p. 53). Arrangement of ideas, he said, should be done prior to the speech and would help the speaker remember what should be said and help the audience follow without confusion. The speaker must also have passion and use emotion in a way that is consistent with his or her thoughts. Misplaced emotion would create discord with the audience.

Blair also addressed delivery, stating that "the best manner of delivery is the firm and the determined" (1965, p. 60). Arrogant and overbearing delivery should be avoided at all costs; a feeble and hesitating manner indicates that the speaker doubts his or her ideas. However, Blair cautioned that effective delivery is not the most important quality of an effective speaker: "To conclude this head, let every Orator remember, that the impression made by fine and artful speaking is momentary; that made by argument and good sense, is solid and lasting" (p. 61). As he did with matters of style, Blair engaged in criticism of ancient orators to illustrate and further elaborate on eloquence, or oratory.

In subsequent lectures on oratory, Blair further examined arrangement, argumentative appeals, delivery, and improving one's skills in public speaking. A speech, he wrote, contained an introduction, stated the subject and facts associated with it, presented arguments, attempted to touch the audience's passions, and contained a conclusion. In terms of argument, Blair addressed the deductive and inductive arguments and emotional proof. When discussing delivery, Blair touched upon tone, emphasis, use of pauses, and other aspects of delivery.

Criticism

Although Blair devotes much of the last thirteen lectures to criticism, he defines the subject in the third lecture. Criticism, to him, was a way of evaluating beauty by using standards that have been established through experience. Blair's style of criticism is far more formal and systematic than anything we have seen so far. Not only does Blair use criticism to illustrate and further explore the points made in his discussion of style, eloquence, and other topics, but he uses criticism for its own sake to investigate matters such as philosophical writing, poetry, and drama. Blair's systematic approach to criticism today most closely resembles literary criticism, rather than rhetorical criticism. But Blair clearly identified the practices and principles that are used by critics in all aspects of the liberal arts today.

Conclusion

In addition to his focus on criticism, Blair developed a theory of rhetoric that focused on style. Blair's work is illustrative of how rhetorical theory progressed from Longinus in the classical ages to the practice of *artes dictaminis* in the Middle Ages. Like St. Augustine, Blair was interested in how pastors could make effective the word of God for their congregations. From Blair's more comprehensive work on rhetorical style, we move to the elocutionary movement.

Section Seven: Sublime

Section Seven: Sublime

On the Sublime

Craig R. Smith

On the Sublime

On the Sublime was once thought to be by Dionysius Cassius Longinus (A.D. 213 to 273) a citizen of Athens who studied Plato and became a teacher of philosophy and rhetoric. Although we are no longer sure about this attribution (sometimes referred to as Psuedo-Longinus), we do know that the work gives us evidence that the theory of *decorum* was alive and well during the Second Sophistic, a time when display and ceremonial speech reigned supreme. Chapter III of *On the Sublime* emphasizes the importance of expectation in the audience, and the author lists the specific means of achieving *decorum* starting in chapter XVI. The book argued that devices which enhanced imagination (*phantasia*) made the real more real, and the true more true for the audience.

But the book seeks more than that. The author wants to teach students "not to persuade the audience but rather to transport them out of themselves." This requires forming "great conceptions" that stimulate the human soul; the orator must "inspire the passions" with "the due formation of figures, . . . noble diction," and "dignified and elevated compositions." The author claimed that sublime prose would cause the orator to be revered in "each succeeding age." He went on to link style to persona: "Sublimity is the echo of a great soul." To heighten this effect, the speaker needs to find a poetic link which can be achieved by combining figures, by majesty of expression, and by the use of elevation, elaboration, and amplification. The sublime stresses the spiritual over the material, and delicacy and grace over the crude and simple.

What we have then is a system of style that transforms the stage of a play or the platform of a speaker into a world that the audience has never seen. It takes them to another time and place. Cicero, Quintilian, and Longinus enriched the three purposes of oratory—to move, to teach, to please—with encouragement to seek the style appropriate to each occasion.

What Is the Sublime?

Timothy Borchers

The **sublime,** according to Longinus, is the use of language to momentarily lift the audience members outside of themselves. He defined the sublime as "The process by which we may raise our natural powers to a required advance in scale" (*On the Sublime,* section I). The sublime was not an appeal to logic, or even emotion, but an appeal to the stylistic and aesthetic faculties of the audience. Longinus traced the sublime to the speaker's use of language: "Subliminity is always an eminence and excellence in language" (section I).

The sublime has a powerful impact on audience. In fact, Longinus placed the sublime ahead of logical, pathetic, or ethical appeals. He argued,

> For it is not to persuasion but to ecstasy that passages of extraordinary genius carry the hearer: now the marvelous, with its power to amaze, is always and necessarily stronger than that which seeks to persuade and to please: to be persuaded rests usually with ourselves, genius brings force sovereign and irresistible to bear upon every hearer, and takes its stand high above him. (section I)
>
> For it is a fact of Nature that the soul is raised by true subliminity, it gains a proud step upwards, it is filled with joy and exultation, as though itself had produced what it hears. (section VI)

According to Longinus, subliminity is remembered, it is impossible to resist, and it promotes reflection on the part of the listener.

Subliminity is more than the manipulation of language, though. To Longinus, subliminity can only be achieved by excellent speakers who possess a "genius" for style. The speaker must know more than how to use the canons of invention and arrangement. Rather, a single passage may reveal the speaker's eloquence and "genius." Longinus states, "Sublimity, we know, brought out at the happy moment, parts all the matter this way and that, and like a lightening flash, reveals, at a stroke and in its entirety, the power of the orator" (section I). After defining the sublime, Longinus explains the dangers of trying to create the sublime without having the natural and artistic ability to do so.

Sources of the Sublime

Longinus saw the sublime as a product of both nature and art. A speaker had to have natural abilities to achieve the sublime, but there were also ways of learning how to create sublimity in a speech. Longinus stressed that natural ability was a primary factor and that artistic elements were secondary. In all, five qualities are necessary for the sublime. Two qualities are natural—passion and great thoughts—and three are the result of artistry—use of figures, diction, and composition. Let's explore the various elements of the sublime.

Natural Qualities Two qualities of the sublime cannot be taught; a speaker must be born with passion and great thoughts. Longinus did not discuss passion at length, but he did notice that some speakers could be sublime without passion, although they are limited in their eloquence. Additionally, the presence of passion does not necessarily make a speaker sublime. Longinus cites examples of Roman orators who were passionate but not sublime. In sum, he explains the role of passion in creating the sublime thus: "I should feel confidence in maintaining that nothing reaches great eloquence so surely as genuine passion in the right place" (section VIII). Likewise, the sublime comes from speakers who have a great mind. Longinus explains,

> The true Orator must have no low ungenerous spirit, for it is not possible that they who think small thoughts, fit for slaves, and practice them in all their daily life, should put out anything to deserve wonder and immortality. Great words issue, and it cannot be otherwise, from those whose thoughts are weighty. So it is on the lips of men of the highest spirit that words of rare greatness are found. (section IX)

Longinus suggested three particular methods of communicating great thoughts: silence, amplification, and appeals to imagination. In some situations, the speaker doesn't have to say anything to communicate a profound thought. Silence, then, is a form of sublimity that speakers with a great mind have mastered. Additionally, amplification—the arrangement of thoughts in ascending order—can be used to create the sublime if it is not done mechanically. That is, amplification must be accompanied by great thoughts and used by a great speaker in order to achieve the sublime. Finally, the ability to use imagination, or to "see the things of which you speak, and place them under the eyes of your hearers" (section X) is the sign of a great mind, according to Longinus.

Artistic Qualities In treating the artistic methods of creating sublimity, Longinus begins with a discussion of the proper use of figures of speech and thought. You'll recall that we briefly discussed rhetorical figures in the previous chapter. Longinus notes that a speaker must handle them properly in order to achieve greatness. There are hundreds of figures of speech and thought that a speaker may use to achieve sublimity. In *On the Sublime* Longinus highlights a few of them.

Asyndeton is achieved by dropping connecting words—such as "and"—from a series of words or statements. Longinus quotes Xenophon for an example: "Locking their shields, they pushed, fought, slew, died." You'll note that the word "and" is not included before the last word in the series, "died." The effect of this rhetorical figure, according to Longinus, is to "carry the impression of a struggle, where the meaning is at once checked and hurried on" (section XIX).

Hyperbaton is a disturbance of the proper sequence of phrases or thoughts. Longinus explains this figure in vivid detail, saying that a speaker may "put forward one set of ideas, then spring aside to another, thrusting in a parenthesis out of all logic, then wheel round to the first, and in their [the audience's] excitement, like a ship before an unsteady gale, drag phrases and thoughts sharply across, now this way, now that" (section XXII). The effect is that the words don't seem to be prepared but that they emerge naturally from the speaker. Longinus cites an example from Dionysius of Phocace, who extolled his audience, "Our fortunes rest on the edge of a razor, O Ionians, whether we are to be free or slaves" (section XXII). Longinus notes that natural order would have been to start with the recognition of the audience—"O Ionians." Then, the speaker would have presented the choice—to be free or slaves—before telling them of the consequence of their choice. By rearranging the natural order, the speaker was more eloquent and more able to achieve the sublime.

Longinus also discusses *periphrasis,* which is the use of plain words to mean something far more elegant. This figure must be handled carefully and is one of the more difficult to use, according to Longinus. Plato, for instance, referred to death as an "appointed journey" and the funeral rites as "a public escort" given by the deceased friends and relatives. Longinus explained that plain speech used in this way creates harmony with the thoughts and eloquent words that surround the plain speech.

The second artistic method of achieving sublimity is diction, or choosing the right words and grand words. Beautiful words, said Longinus, are "the light of thought" (section XXX), but they must be chosen and used carefully. Using grand words in places where they do not fit would be similar to fastening "a large tragic mask upon a little child" (section XXX). Particular care should be taken when employing metaphors. Longinus explained that two or three, at the most, are appropriate for a subject. As with all elements of sublimity, proportion is key. A speech that takes on too many ornamental elements does not achieve greatness, or sublimity.

Finally, Longinus addressed the issue of composition, which is the arrangement of words. The correct ordering of words creates rhythm, melody, and beauty: "Composition, I say, must by all these means at once soothe us as we hear and also dispose to stateliness, and high mood, and sublimity" (section XXXIX). Among the elements of composition that detract from sublimity are broken rhythm, excessive conciseness of expression, and words that sound poorly when placed together.

Conclusion

Longinus's *On the Sublime* was reportedly written in 200 C.E. The book details a specific way of using rhetoric to achieve style, eloquence, and sublimity. For nearly a thousand years after the book was written, rhetorical scholars were influenced by his treatment of style and considered style as one of the most important canons of rhetoric. For a contemporary example of Longinus's view of sublime rhetoric, read the Critical Insight box for this chapter (see Box 3.1). As we continue our discussion below, you'll continue to see how style dominated the study of rhetoric.

SECTION EIGHT: THE EPISTEMOLOGISTS

SECTION EIGHT

The Epistemologists

James Golden

We place those authors in the psychological-philosophical or epistemological school of thought whose principal concern was to relate communication theory to the basic nature of man. With determination and skill, reinforced by painstaking research in the natural and social sciences, they set for themselves the task of unraveling the mystery of man's mind and soul. Notwithstanding the fact that their fame was derived primarily from writings generally associated with psychology and philosophy, these epistemologists left an indelible imprint upon the direction rhetoric was to take for generations to come.

Our discussion of this trend will be divided into two parts. First we will deal with four great innovators of Western thought who made their contributions during the period from 1600 to 1725: Francis Bacon, René Descartes, John Locke, and Giambattista Vico. What these great thinkers had to say about the knowledge in general and communication theory in particular remains provocative and challenging to contemporary students.

We then move on to the 18th Century Epistomologists.

The Four Innovators, 1600–1725

Francis Bacon

Shortly after Copernicus made the startling discovery that the earth with clockwise precision rotates around the sun; his European followers—including Kepler, Gilbert, Galileo, Bacon, Descartes, and Boyle—initiated a scientific movement that challenged the classical preoccupation with deduction, and stressed the value of an experimental method based on the inductive process. Of this group of modern thinkers, Bacon and Descartes had the most impact on rhetoric. Described as "the greatest poet of science" and the "herald of the scientific movement," Bacon, who had come to realize the importance of the recent discoveries—"printing, gunpowder, and the compass"—recommended to his contemporaries "a total reform of human knowledge, a true advancement of learning, and a revolution in the conditions of life."[1] Convinced that progress was an inherent principle of life, he sketched in 1605 a philosophy of optimism in his first monumental work, the "Advancement of Learning." In this treatise may be found Bacon's innovative discussion of the faculties of the mind.[2] "The parts of human learning," he argued, "have reference to the three parts of Man's Understanding which is the seat of learning: History to his Memory, Poesy to his Imagination, and Philosophy to his Reason."[3] To the faculties of understanding, reason, imagination, and memory, he then added will and appetite. These categories explaining the mind of man led to Bacon's celebrated statement that "the duty and office of Rhetoric is to *apply Reason* to *Imagination* for the better moving of the will."[4]

An integral part of Bacon's rhetorical theory was his concept of invention. Unlike the ancients, he played down the role of discovery in the formulation of arguments and the gathering of source data, emphasizing instead the element of "remembrance." A speaker, in effect, reaches back into his memory to summon forth knowledge that he already knows; then he applies it to the rhetorical situation at hand.[5]

How, it might be asked, does the communicator get the knowledge that is to be stored in the memory for appropriate use in a given situation? Bacon's response to this question is both traditional and original. He is strikingly similar to the classical scholars in suggesting that knowledge may be obtained from general and special or particular topics. But he is innovative in his discussion of four commonplaces as aids to invention. The first, he calls *"Colours of Good and Evil."* "The persuader's labour," Bacon argues, "is to make things appear good or evil, and that in higher or lower degree. . . ."[6] To assist potential speakers in the use of this commonplace, Bacon provided a "Table of Colours or appearances of Good and Evil" which contains shades of meaning and a list of possible accompanying fallacies associated with a particular argument.[7] Since the commonplace of "Colours of Good and Evil" often deals with premises that appear on the surface to be true, Bacon warns us to examine such claims critically. Consider, for instance, the following statement: "What men praise and honour is good; what they dispraise and condemn is evil." At first glance the thought expressed in this argument seems to be a high level "good" grounded in the idea that public sentiment is infallible. But to Bacon this argument is a sophism which deceives people by appealing to their ignorance, factional spirit, prejudices, and "natural disposition" to "praise and blame."[8]

The second commonplace, which is labeled "antitheta," consists of theses which may be argued pro and con. In his *De augmentis*, Bacon lists forty-seven theses expressed both in affirmative and negative terms. Similar to a modern day debate brief, this technique helps the advocate answer possible objections to his claims; it is also useful in making decisions. Assume, for example, that we are confronted with the difficult and challenging task of rendering a decision on a controversial issue. If we use Bacon's method of "antitheta," we might take a sheet of paper, draw a vertical line down the middle of the page, and then place the affirmative contentions on the left side and the negative counter claims on the right. By weighing all of the arguments for and against, Bacon implies, we should be able to reach a thoughtful conclusion.

"Formulae" constitute a third type of commonplace or aid to invention. They are "small parts of a speech, fully composed and ready for use. . . ."[9] They may take the form of a stock phrase, sentence, or paragraph designed to serve as a transition or summary; or a humorous thrust devised for the purpose of blunting the attack or image of an adversary. Here Bacon, perhaps drawing upon his own rich experience in law courts and in Parliament, illustrates how "formulae" may be employed to diminish the impact of an opponent's argument. "When one's adversary declares, 'you go from the matter,' you reply: 'But it was to follow you.' When he demands that 'you come to the point,' you answer: 'Why, I shall not find you there.' If he says, 'You take more than is for granted,' you retort: 'You grant less than is proved.'"[10] Admittedly, such examples appear contrived and artificial. But this kind of rhetorical strategy is still prevalent in contemporary political, forensic, and religious discourse.

The fourth and final commonplace discussed by Bacon is that of *"apothegms."* These are "pointed speeches" or pithy statements which may be "interlaced in continued speech" or "recited upon occasion of themselves." Like salt, they can be "sprinkled where you will."[11] In compiling a list of "apothegms," Bacon alluded to the classics, British and continental history, and to his own works. The ensuing examples are representative:

- When the oracle of Delphi pronounced Socrates to be the wisest man in Greece, Socrates is reputed to have said: "I am not wise, and know it; others are not wise, and know it not."
- "Queen Isabella of Spain used to say, 'Whosoever hath a good presence and a good fashion, carries continual letters of recommendation.'"[12]

Nor was Bacon content to describe the nature and utility of the commonplaces; he also gave three useful hints for collecting them. First, he asserted, we should *observe* the world around us, taking special note of particular instances, similarities and contrasts in events, and the "utterances of others."[13] Secondly, we should *converse* freely in order to generate fresh insights. The well-known political leaders—Charles James Fox of the eighteenth century and Robert Kennedy of our own—relied on this method, more than any other, for gaining the knowledge needed to cope with knotty domestic and international problems. Thirdly, Bacon adds, we should *study* widely, especially in the area of history.

Bacon next turns to a consideration of how to record the data gathered from the process of observing, conversing, and studying. His advice was the use of commonplace "note books or phrase books." To make certain that the source material in these books be etched in the memory, Bacon suggested: "One man's notes will little profit another. . . . "[14] The act of writing one's own notes, he felt, contributed importantly to the practice of recall. Among those contemporary figures we have known who used a commonplace book for preparation of speeches was John F. Kennedy.

Perhaps more vital in appreciating Bacon's contribution to knowledge is to examine his analysis of sense perception. Motivated by a desire to establish progressive stages of certainty, he rejected the widely practiced inductive method that moved from particular instances to general premises, and then proceeded to "judgment and the discovery of middle axioms." Instead, he observed, we should derive "axioms from the senses and particulars, rising by a gradual and unbroken ascent, so that it arrives at the most general axioms last of all."[15] Bacon's interest in psychology led him to conclude that faulty sense perception could hinder man's quest for establishing reliable and valid conclusions through the method of induction. He was particularly concerned with the need to clear the human mind of four potential fallacies which he called the "Idols of the Tribe," "Idols of the Cave," "Idols of the Market Place," and "Idols of the Theatre."[16] These terms used to designate the fallacies were both novel and meaningful. The "Idols of the Tribe" represented the inherent limitations in the general nature of man. As a whole, suggested Bacon, mankind shared a homogeneous spirit that often exemplifies obsessions, narrowness, restlessness, and excessive emotionality. Moreover it is a spirit formed in part by an inadequate response to sense messages that may be blurred or inaccurate. Thus it is wrong, asserted Bacon, to argue "that the sense of man is the measure of things."[17]

If the "Idols of the Tribe" stem from human nature itself as seen in the generality of man, the "Idols of the Cave" are derived from those unique qualities and experiences of the individual man. One's basic personality, intellectual capacity, educational training, occupation, or value system may serve as "a cave or den of his own, which refracts, and discolours the light of nature."[18] The life style that results from these elements significantly affects an individual's attempt to interpret his sense impressions.

Not only is a man influenced by his general and particular nature, but by his close associations with others in the "Market Place." Here Bacon, anticipating the twentieth-century semanticist, warned of the pitfalls confronting those who failed to use words with precision and care while communicating with others. Such writers and speakers, he said, confuse words with things, and hastily conceived definitions with reality. This idol, consequently, is the most troublesome fallacy because "the ill and unfit choice of words wonderfully obstructs the understanding."[19]

The final idol, that of the Theatre, describes how untested information that has "immigrated into men's minds from the various dogmas of philosophy, and also from wrong laws of demonstration," are "but so many stage plays, representing worlds of their own creation after an unreal and scenic fashion."[20] Bacon used this idol to attack those philosophical systems that have been handed down from generation to generation with no effort on the part of the recipients to apply scientific criteria for the purpose of judging their validity.

To conclude his perceptive analysis of the idols, Bacon stressed its meaning for his theory of knowledge. Since his purpose was to construct an epistemological system that would lead men to an earthly kingdom "founded on the sciences," he saw the idols as barriers that would block the entrance. Thus these fallacies "must be renounced and put away with a fixed and solemn determination, and the understanding thoroughly freed and cleansed." In fine, man in search of scientific certainty must assume the purity and simplicity of a little child which Christianity holds to be essential for "entrance into the kingdom of heaven."[21]

To gain further insight into Bacon's notions on the Idols, consider the following passage drawn from his *Novum organum:*

> There are four classes of Idols which beset men minds. To these for distinction's sake I have assigned names—calling the first class *Idols of the Tribe;* the second, *Idols of the Cave;* the third, *Idols of the Marketplace;* the fourth, *Idols of the Theatre.*
>
> The formulation of ideas and axioms by true induction is no doubt the proper remedy to be applied for the keeping off and clearing away of idols. To point them out, however, is of great use; for the doctrine of Idols is to the interpretation of Nature what the doctrine of the refutation of Sophisms is to common logic.

> The Idols of the Tribe have their foundation in human nature itself and in the tribe or race of men. For it is a false assertion that the sense of man is the measure of things. On the contrary, all perceptions as well of the sense as of the mind are according to the measure of the universe. And the human understanding is like a false mirror, which, receiving rays irregularly, distorts and discolours the nature of things by mingling its own nature with it.
>
> The Idols of the Cave are the idols of the individual man. For everyone (besides the errors common to human nature in general) have a cave or den of his own, which refracts and discolours the light of nature; owing either to his own proper and peculiar nature; or to his education and conversation with others; or to the reading of books, and the authority of those whom he esteems and admires; or to the differences of impressions, accordingly as they take place in a mind preoccupied and predisposed or in a mind indifferent and settled; or the like. So that the spirit of man (according as it is meted out to different individuals) is in fact a thing variable and full of perturbation, and governed as it were by chance. Whence it was well observed by Heraclitus that men look for sciences in their own lesser worlds, and not in the greater or common world.
>
> There are also idols formed by the intercourse and association of men with each other, which I call Idols of the Marketplace, on account of the commerce and consort of men there. For it is by discourse that men associate; and words are imposed according to the apprehension of the vulgar. And therefore the ill and unfit choice of words wonderfully obstructs the understanding. Nor do the definitions or explanations wherewith in some things learned men are wont to guard and defend themselves, by any means set the matter right. But words plainly force and overrule the understanding, and throw all into confusion, and lead men away into numberless empty controversies and idle fancies.
>
> Lastly, there are idols which have immigrated into men's minds from the various dogmas of philosophies, and also from wrong laws of demonstration. These I call Idols of the Theatre; because in my judgment all the received systems are but so many stage-plays, representing worlds of their own creation after an unreal and scenic fashion. Nor is it only of the systems now in vogue, or only of the ancient sects and philosophies, that I speak; for many more plays of the same kind may yet be composed and in like artificial manner set forth; seeing that errors the most widely different have nevertheless causes for the most part alike. Neither again do I mean this only of entire systems, but also of many principles and axioms in science, which by tradition, credulity, and negligence have come to be received.

Two other aspects of Bacon's philosophy are not without significance for the role they played in helping to mold eighteenth-century rhetorical theory. First was his rejection of the syllogism as a productive means for establishing principles. That the syllogism with its emphasis on opinion and probability and its usefulness in checking reasoning was important to popular arts such as rhetoric, Bacon was willing to admit. Indeed, he, like Aristotle, recognized the function of topics and commonplaces in constructing arguments. But he excluded the syllogism as a part of his scientific method on the grounds that it had little correspondence to the essential nature of things. He put it this way in his essay on "The Great Instauration," written in 1620—fifteen years after "The Advancement of Learning."

> The syllogism consists of propositions; propositions of words; and words are the tokens and signs of notions. Now if the very notions of the mind . . . be improperly and overhastily abstracted from facts, vague, not sufficiently definite, faulty in short in many ways, the whole edifice tumbles. I therefore reject the syllogism; and that not only as regards principles . . . but also as regards middle propositions; which, although obtainable no doubt by the syllogism, are, when so obtained, barren of works, remote from practice, and altogether unavailable for the active department of the sciences. Although therefore I leave to the syllogism and these famous and boasted modes of demonstration their jurisdiction over popular arts and such as are matter of opinion (in which department I leave all as it is), yet in dealing with the nature of things I use induction throughout, and that in the minor propositions as well as the major. For I consider induction to be that form of demonstration which upholds the sense, and closes with nature, and comes to the very brink of operation, if it does not actually deal with it.[22]

In later discussions we will observe how Bacon's reservations concerning the syllogism prepared the way for similar attacks by Descartes, Locke, Hume, and Campbell.

Secondly, it is instructive to note that Bacon was among the early English prose authors who sought to replace the copious style, then in vogue, with a language control featuring Attic simplicity. He was content to break with the Elizabethan tradition even though it led to a "schizm of eloquence" because of his conviction that scientific ideas may best be expressed in a clear, unadorned style.[23] Bacon thus contributed importantly to the doctrine of perspicuity that was to become a benchmark of eighteenth century rhetorical thought.

Bacon's pioneering theories set into motion a movement toward a new empiricism that achieved focus and symbolic effect in the experimental studies of the Royal Society. In his history of the Society published in the 1660s, Thomas Sprat eulogized Bacon for providing the inspiration and direction of his "Enterprize, as it is now set on foot. . . ."[24] Additionally he praised him for his cogent defense of "Experimental Philosophy" and his model of excellence in style. Sprat's assessment of Bacon's accomplishments has been widely shared by subsequent writers.

René Descartes

While the theories of Bacon and the Royal Society were being disseminated throughout England, similar probings into the nature of man and methods of study were taking place in France. These inquiries began in earnest in 1637 with the publication of Descartes' celebrated *Discourse on Method.* Partly autobiographical, this study contains the heart of Descartes' philosophy. He relates that when he had completed his studies, he resolved to devote his remaining years to an analysis of himself rather than to the reading of books. By then, however, Descartes already had formed strong convictions concerning branches of learning that were a part of the humane tradition. He regarded "eloquence highly, and was in raptures with poesy (i.e. poetry)," but thought that "both were gifts of nature rather than fruits of study."[25] He complained that the syllogism was incapable of investigating the unknown and separating truth from error. It was, instead, useful only in communicating "what we already know."[26] Most of all, he was "delighted with the mathematics, on account of the certitude and evidence of their reasonings."[27] The remarkable similarity between these views and those expressed by George Campbell in his *Philosophy of Rhetoric* will be observed later.

This preference for mathematical certainty as opposed to syllogistic probability may be seen in Descartes' four-fold study method. With unwavering resolution he was determined to accept only those claims which could be verified with proof containing no ground for doubt; to divide all difficult aspects of a subject into as many segments as possible; to follow a pattern of inquiry utilizing a climactic order and a cause to effect sequence; and to use an all-inclusive system of enumeration that prevents omissions.[28]

Central to Descartes' study design was his faith in the power of reason to determine truth and to discipline the imagination. The mind of man, he suggested, was capable of reaching unchallenged conclusions such as: "I think, therefore I am"; and "God exists." Similarly the mind had the ability to regulate the senses in such a way that the fallacy of the idols could be brought under control. Like Bacon, he further believed in an advancement of learning made possible for an enlightened society through the means of experiments.[29] But he went beyond his predecessor's grasp of understanding abstract scientific principles and in appreciating the full implications of rationalism for the experimental process.[30]

Despite his apparent indebtedness to Bacon, Descartes was, in many respects, unique and prophetic. In arguing that experiment takes precedence over disputation, inquiry over communication, and action over speculation, he broke with the logicians of the past.[31] His mathematical contribution to science and his stress on reasoning enabled him to make bold predictions "which became the assumptions of nineteenth-century science."[32] This overall impact prompted Leon Roth to observe that the *Discourse on Method* "marks an epoch. It is a dividing line in the history of thought. Everything that came before it is old; everything that came after it is new."[33] What is more relevant for this study is the fact that Descartes' work influenced the direction and thrust of the French Academy and, indeed, became a textbook for the Port-Royal logicians and rhetoricians who, in turn, influenced British thought.

Descartes' impact on later scholars can best be seen by turning to the publication of the second edition of Arnauld and Nicole's *Logique of Port-Royal.* This provocative edition contained from the beginning to end the cardinal tenets of Cartesian philosophy and shook the foundations of traditional rhetorical theory. With Descartes and Boileau, Arnauld and Nicole held that truth is the transcendent goal in life. Thus the only acceptable communication model is one which adheres to the principles of geometry requiring demonstration based on clear definitions, axioms, and cause to effect relations. In such a system there could be no place for the scholastic art of syllogizing, commonplaces which substitute verisimilitude for reality, or highly emotional appeals. Nor was there a need for a method of expression or invention because of man's natural facility in these areas. In short, since rhetoric cannot produce truth it is, at best, relegated to the simple task of communicating principles that logic and experimentation can discover.[34] These views, as we shall later note, produced a strong counter response from the brilliant Italian scholar, Giambattista Vico.

John Locke

Many of the ideas of Bacon and Descartes, as well as those of the members of the French Academy and Royal Society, found eloquent expression in John Locke's monumental *Essay Concerning Human Understanding* written in 1690. To a large extent Locke succeeded in summarizing the central features of seventeenth-century scientific thought. Additionally, however, he presented novel and penetrating insights into the nature of man. Although Locke is well known for his claim that rhetoric was a "powerful Instrument of Error and Deceit,"[35] he had a positive influence on the psychological-philosophical theories of discourse that evolved in the eighteenth century, culminating in Campbell's *Philosophy of Rhetoric*. Of the many concepts included in Locke's *Essay*, four have special meaning for students of rhetorical theory. They are his treatment of the faculties of the mind, association of ideas, pathetic proof, and the syllogism.

Locke concluded that since the mind has the power to *perceive* and *prefer*, it must be comprised of two major faculties, the understanding and the will.[36] In explaining the nature of the faculty of understanding, Locke developed his famous theory of ideas. Reflection upon sensory experience, he observed, produces ideas which are, in turn, held together in a meaningful pattern through the talent of the mind to trace relationships that show natural correspondence and connection. Reason likewise enables us to unite ideas that are apparently unrelated by relying on the laws of association. Here we may observe from past experiences that whenever a particular idea reaches the understanding an "associate appears with it." Under such conditions, the doctrine of association permits us to connect these concepts so that they will form an inseparable unit in our minds.[37]

Locke's thesis caused him to reject the syllogism on the grounds that it neither demonstrates nor strengthens the connection that two ideas may have with each other. Nor does it advance an argument or lead to moral truth. The power of inference, a gift presented to man by God, makes it possible for us to perceive associations and to determine whether or not ideas are coherent or incoherent. Thus the understanding, concludes Locke, "is not taught to reason" by the "methods of syllogizing."[38] Quite clearly Locke gave a new dimension to the reservations pertaining to the syllogism articulated by Bacon, Descartes, and the Port-Royal logicians.

As one of the early proponents of faculty psychology, Locke came to believe that an idea which reaches the understanding does not necessarily have the power to motivate the will. The rational process, he argued, must be reinforced by a pathetic appeal that ultimately becomes the major determinant of action. All of the emotions have one common element which Locke called "uneasiness," and described as the absence of some good. Whenever the mind experiences "uneasiness," it feels pain and generates the compelling desire to remove it. The will, in short, may be influenced when the passions are stirred, for the arousal of an emotion inevitably causes pain. There is little opportunity for persuasion, however, if the mind is at ease since the desire for happiness has already been achieved.[39] To some extent Locke's views anticipated the twentieth-century theory of cognitive dissonance.[40]

Giambattista Vico

By the time Locke's probings into the human mind had attracted attention in England and on the continent, another European epistemologist, the Italian rhetorician and social scientist Giambattista Vico was elaborating his theory of ideas at the University of Naples .[41] Launching his career in 1699, he immediately began a series of annual lectures which formed the germinal seed of his innovative philosophy.[42] Steeped in the classics—especially in the works of Homer, Plato, Cicero, and the Roman historian, Tacitus—Vico turned to the origin of language and to ancient rhetoric and poetics as a starting point in his quest to unlock the mysteries of man's nature, culture, and history. When he wished to improve his own style, "on successive days he would study Cicero side by side with Boccaccio, Virgil with Dante, and Horace with Petrarch, being curious to see and judge for himself the differences between them."[43] But the two classicists he admired above all others were Plato and Tacitus. He explains this preference in the following manner: "For with an incomparable metaphysical mind Tacitus contemplates man as he is, Plato as he should be,"[44] In the writings of these two ancient authors, Vico saw the model he hoped to imitate—that which presented both the virtues of pragmatism and idealism.

But if he derived much of his early basic philosophy and method from Plato and Tacitus, he received his greatest help in the area of communication from Homer and Cicero. From the readings of Homer who represented much of the early knowledge of the Greeks, Vico first saw a close relationship between rhetoric and human nature. Man alone, he came to believe, knows with a high degree of accuracy his own feelings and attitudes and expresses these sentiments to others with a wide range of universal communication procedures such as verbal and nonverbal symbols, art, and music. Since people of all ages adhere to this practice of communicating a language that can be interpreted, each person through sympathy can know, at least approximately, the feelings of his contemporaries. Equally important, by studying the communicative patterns of earlier societies, one may similarly come to appreciate what they have believed and experienced.[45]

The prime source of Vico's rhetorical theory was Cicero who held that rhetoric is a useful art designed to help men adjust to the exigencies of life, thereby rendering them more productive and influential. It was Cicero who taught him that rhetoric, a form of practical knowledge based on probability, is as significant in the sphere of human relations and conduct as a mathematical truth stemming from geometry is to the physical world.

Cicero's orations, moreover, persuaded him that the generality of mankind cannot be motivated unless the passions are stirred.[46] Most of all, it was Cicero who convinced him that verisimilitudes constructed from topics or lines of arguments, rather than a recitation of physical facts, constituted the pivotal element needed to alter one's behavior through speech.[47]

Vico, it would appear, equated invention with the topics, and regarded the Ciceronian theory of the verisimilar with its emphasis on probability as the key to knowledge.[48] He did so with the conviction that "absolute truth, as preached by the Cartesians, does not appeal to all the faculties of the mind."[49] By supplanting certainty with verisimilitude, Vico pointed the way to the social scientist's use of the concept of "hypothesis," and "illustrated the practical end toward which knowledge should tend."[50]

Up to this point the analysis tends to suggest that Vico was an uncompromising classicist who was preoccupied with the obsession to use ancient doctrines to diminish the appeal of Descartes and other seventeenth-century modernists. Such an assessment is not responsive to the evidence. For Vico's early devotion to Homer, Plato, Tacitus, and Cicero was matched by his later zeal for Bacon. Indeed, he found the "esoteric wisdom" of Plato and the "common wisdom" of Tacitus both present in the comprehensive and ingenious mind of Bacon.[51] After making this discovery, he developed an abiding belief in the premise that the "constant of human nature" could be "reduced to scientific principles."[52] He admired the successes of Galileo and Newton in systematizing and explaining the scientific characteristics inherent in the world of nature, and became convinced that he could, by using the tools of social and behavioral science, discover similar valid axioms pertaining to the world of nations.[53] What he found was to have far-reaching significance for historiography and anthropology. His researches led him to conclude that there was "an ideal eternal history traversed in time by the history of every nation in its rise, development, maturity, decline, and fall."[54] In observing that every nation goes through a series of stages beginning with inception and concluding with disintegration, Vico became the first major proponent of the cyclical view of history.[55] Moreover, in suggesting that a society begins with a primitive belief in magic and progresses to an advanced commitment to philosophy, he gave support to the sociological tenet that nature is not static, but an ongoing process of growth. Whatever occurs in the historical evolution of a nation, therefore, takes place at the appropriate point in the cyclical pattern.[56]

After Vico had established the essential principles of his new science, he enthusiastically compared it with the natural sciences. In fact, he was willing to argue that the geometrical propositions which Descartes and his followers held to be the key to our understanding of the physical world were merely creations of man. It is easy, concluded Vico, to demonstrate mathematical principles because they are man-made concepts designed to conform to our perception of the universe. As such, these propositions are no more reliable than the knowledge derived from scientific historical methods depicting the story of man.[57] In thus avoiding the polarities of rationalism on the one hand and empiricism on the other, Vico developed for himself the task of providing a synthesis of the two approaches to knowledge.

At this juncture it is useful to summarize the arguments which Vico used in his attempt to refute some of the major tenets advanced in Descartes' *Discourse on Method.* To make these ideas salient, we present the brief on the preceding page containing the central arguments both of Descartes and of Vico. Three points should be remembered as you examine Descartes' contentions and Vico's rejoinder. First, the sequence of the arguments has been determined by us in order to ensure clarity and to see appropriate relationships. Secondly, Vico, in constructing his response approximately seven decades after Descartes had written his treatise, had the advantage of hindsight. Thirdly, it is of interest to note that the opposing views articulated here are often reproduced in the 1990s with a group of philosophers on one side and the rhetoricians on the other.

The immediate failure of Vico to attract widespread support for his creative attempt to synthesize classical and modem precepts is surprising. René Wellek has argued that Vico's supposed impact on England and Scotland in the eighteenth century is, at best, marginal.[58] Yet so pervasive was his influence on the social sciences during the nineteenth and twentieth centuries that Sir Isaiah Berlin—President of Oriel College at Oxford—calls him "one of the boldest innovators in the history of human thought." Berlin further adds that Vico virtually invented the idea of culture; his theory of mathematics has to wait until our own century to be recognized as revolutionary; he anticipated the esthetics of both romantics and historicists, and almost transformed the subject; he virtually invented comparative anthropology and philology and inaugurated the new approach to history and the social sciences that this entailed; his notions of language, myth, law, symbolism, and the relationship of social to cultural evolution, embodied insights of genius; he first drew that celebrated distinction between the natural sciences and human studies that has remained a crucial issue ever since.[59] When it is remembered that Vico's social science philosophy was developed during his long tenure as a Professor of

Rhetoric at the University of Naples, his status as a pioneering communication theorist is remarkable. To him we are indebted for his reaffirmation of the role of probability in rhetoric and for his brilliant attempt to place rhetoric squarely in the tradition of the emerging field of social and behavioral science.

Summary

It is difficult to overestimate the impact that Bacon, Descartes, Locke, and Vico had on the development of rhetorical thought. Approaching their study of the nature of man from similar starting points, they did not always reach the same conclusions. This was particularly true of Descartes who alone among the four innovators tended to embrace a form of absolutism patterned on the model of mathematics. Yet Descartes was an influential figure in the history of British and continental rhetorical theory because he created a rhetorical situation which demanded Vico's response upholding the value of probability and the integrity of the social sciences. Taken as a whole the imaginative writings of these epistemologists served as a model and inspiration for later authors representing the psychological-philosophical school of rhetoric.

Eighteenth-Century Epistemologists

At the time of Vico's death in 1744, the philosophy of rationalism, which had received its major impetus from the writings of Descartes and Locke, began to take hold among many of the leading literati in Britain and on the continent. In varying degrees the works of David Hume, David Hartley, Lord Kames, Adam Smith, Joseph Priestley, Samuel Johnson, Edward Gibbon, François Voltaire, Jean Jacques Rousseau, and Thomas Paine reflect this emphasis. As rationalism unfolded in the eighteenth century there were three clearly delineated features. First, there was a heightened consciousness for the need of logic in the study of man and his institutions. Secondly, there was an absolute belief in the attainability of reliable knowledge. Thirdly, there was a faith in the capacity of man to make society better. Reason, in sum, was no longer the property of philosophers but a weapon for social improvement.[60]

The telltale signs of rationalistic thought were highly visible. Despite the enormous appeal of traditional Christianity promulgated by John Wesley, religion, for instance, contracted sharply in the eighteenth century. Prior to 1660, the world was viewed as a place of sin, peopled with men who were wicked. God and the devil haunted man. But from 1660 onward religion was less influential. The messages of Bishop Tillotson reflected changing attitudes induced by rationalism. To him, religion was a matter of right behavior; and since there was nothing evil in riches, places, or profits, the world was a happy spot in which to live.[61] As the ideas of rationalism began to secularize society, many prominent thinkers embraced a highly generalized deism. Some felt that they no longer had a need to look to God; others made a polite nod to the unknown. It was against this background of declining interest in orthodox religion in the latter part of the century that Hugh Blair delivered his popular sermons at St. Giles Church in Edinburgh.[62] The fact that Blair gained such prominence as a Protestant divine was not due to his eloquence or to his grasp of theology, but to his talent to construct relevant and inoffensive moral discourses that kept alive the latent religious sentiment of his audience.[63]

Another sign of the steadily increasing impact of rationalism was its influence in governmental and social affairs. In the 1690s Locke and Newton advised the government on currency affairs. Of still greater significance was the fact that a realistic attitude toward experimentalism developed. Statistics were used in decision-making, and a rational approach to social and economic matters began to be introduced.

A third sign could be observed in the continued advance of the scientific revolution which had been initiated in the seventeenth century. Even though there was an active decline in the number of scientists by 1730, science nevertheless continued to move forward. By the 1740s and 1750s scientific societies and lectures prepared for large popular audiences became the order of the day. These public discourses were designed for adults who wished to explore the physical world through scientific methods. The undiminished thirst for knowledge produced an age of circulating libraries, encyclopedias, and dictionaries.[64] In addition, it brought on an era in which young people alarmed their elders by wanting to read radical writers like Thomas Paine.[65] It was the age of Josiah Wedgwood's scientific approach to pottery-making—an enterprise whose products stand for quality to this very day.

To what extent did the rhetoricians make use of the basic tenets of rationalism? How did they view the classical tradition? What were the immediate and long range influences of this modern epistemology on the rhetoric of Western thought? The answers to these questions should provide an insight into what might be called the eighteenth-century British version of the psychological-philosophical theory of discourse.

One of the distinguishing characteristics of the rationalists, as noted earlier, was a compelling desire to study human nature. Their probings convinced them of man's *unique* power, to engage in abstract thought and to communicate on the level of symbolism. To understand the mind of man, they came to believe, was to recognize the nature and function of discourse. Consequently, writers of diverse orientation developed a considerable interest in rhetoric. The works of David Hume and David Hartley, in particular, demonstrate how a philosopher and a physician could be rhetoricians.

Before proceeding to an analysis of the theories of the British epistemologists, we should observe briefly their method and sources. With a goal to construct a rhetoric consistent with the principles of man's nature, they brought to their task a knowledge of and appreciation for the elements of classicism that had a permanent relevance, and precepts of modernism that possess contemporary scientific and social value. They were, in essence, synthesizers who applied scholarly criteria in evaluating the worth of all information handed down to them. In doing so, they strove hard to free themselves from the four fallacies of sensory experience and educational training outlined by Bacon.

The principal British epistemologists concerned with rhetoric were David Hume, David Hartley, Lord Kames, Joseph Priestley, George Campbell, and Richard Whately. Although we will discuss each of these representative authors, far greater attention will be given to Campbell and Whately because of the substantial influence they exercised. Thus, a later chapter will be devoted to their theories and contributions.

David Hume

If John Locke was the pillar of rational thought, David Hume, a close disciple, was the leading world philosopher and interpreter of humanism to write in English.[66] In any analysis of the writings of Hume it is important to remember that he, like his associates Blair and Campbell, was a native of Scotland—a small country which experienced "unrivaled literary brilliance" during the period from 1739 to 1783.[67] Among those who initiated the "second golden age" of Scottish letters were Hume and Thomas Reid in philosophy, William Robertson in history, Adam Smith in political economy, Robert Burns in poetry, and Sir Joshua Reynolds in art. The hub of Scottish literary activity was the capital city of Edinburgh. Described by contemporary observers as "a hotbed of genius" and the "Athens of the North."[68] Edinburgh was a cultural center which could take just pride in its celebrated educational institution, the University of Edinburgh. To city and college came students from England, America, and the continent. Thus Blair was able to write to Hume on July 1, 1764: "Our education here is at present in high reputation. The English are crowding down upon us every season."[69]

To Hume must go the major credit for setting the literary revolution in motion. In 1739 he wrote his greatest work, *A Treatise on Human Nature.* Within a few years he published *An Enquiry Concerning Human Understanding* and *An Enquiry Concerning the Principles of Morals.* In these psychological-philosophical works, Hume showed a remarkable capacity to synthesize classical and modern thought, and to generate fresh ideas. Just as Vico had combined a devotion to Plato and Tacitus with an enthusiasm for Bacon, Hume traced his intellectual heritage to Cicero and Locke. Early in his career Hume turned to the writings of Cicero for both instruction and entertainment.[70] Nursing this interest throughout his life, he freely included quotations from and footnotes to Cicero's moral essays, rhetorical works, and orations. By 1742 he had become so familiar with Cicero's speeches that he wrote a critique of them in a letter to Henry Home (Lord Kames).[71] In his *Enquiry Concerning the Principles of Morals* published a few years later, he used a lengthy excerpt from *De Oratore* to illustrate his theory of virtue; and he patterned his *Dialogues* so closely after the model of *De Natura Deorum* that he all but lost his originality.[72] It is not surprising, therefore, that he could at the middle of the century take comfort in affirming that "the fame of Cicero flourishes at present; but that of Aristotle is utterly decayed."[73]

What makes Hume a central figure in the history of British rhetorical thought, however, was not his admiration for Cicero, but his strong pull toward Locke's philosophy of ideas. He was intrigued by Locke's tendency to compartmentalize the faculties, his theory of association, and his belief in the primacy of the emotions. The teachings of Locke and the example of Isaac Newton, who achieved far-reaching success in applying the experimental method to natural science, spurred Hume to become "the first to put the whole science of man upon an empirical footing, and to appeal to experience exclusively and systematically in teaching his results."[74] The researches that ensued led him to probe the innermost workings of the mind and to devise a theory of reasoning adapted to human nature. What we will find in this analysis is that Hume laid the groundwork for the epistemological approach in Britain in the eighteenth century. So successful was he in achieving his goal that he set the standard for later writers, particularly George Campbell, to follow.

The Nature of the Mind

As he undertook the task of dissecting the nature of the mind, Hume centered his attention on the major areas that are of importance to students of rhetoric.

- two perceptions of the mind
- four faculties
- doctrine of association

Perceptions of the Mind

Hume held that the mind is characterized by two classes or species, which he called ideas or thoughts, and impressions. Ranking these perceptions according to degree of force, he noted that ideas often are abstract, faint, and obscure; and have little vivacity and motivating power. By contrast, impressions are lively concepts that enable us to "hear, or see, or feel, or love, or hate, or desire, or will."[75]

One of the more insightful points emphasized by Hume was his contention that since "ideas are nothing but copies of impressions,"[76] it "is impossible for us to *think* of anything which we have not antecedently *felt*, either by our external or internal senses."[77] Similarly whenever we are confused about the meaning of a term, we are obligated to search for the impression that gave birth to the idea. In sum, an idea, which by its nature lacks force and liveliness, must at all times be clearly associated with a particular impression, the characteristics of which are dynamic and moving sensations. The distinction that we have drawn here between these two concepts will again be evident as we turn to a consideration of the four faculties of the mind highlighted by Hume.

Faculties of the Mind

In his *Enquiry*, Hume repeatedly refers to what he believes to be the four faculties of the mind—understanding, imagination, passions, and the will. The first and fourth of these faculties, as we earlier noted, were stressed by Locke. By treating imagination and the passions as the second and third elements respectively, Hume was convinced that men and women are affective as well as cognitive beings. This suggests that a speaker who wishes to be persuasive must stimulate all of the faculties.

The faculty of understanding is concerned with ideas that are well developed, "clear and determinate," and epitomized by carefully-drawn distinctions between terms. One who instructs in the area of the mathematical sciences limits his rhetorical goal primarily to an informative appeal to the understanding. But a rhetor who seeks to address the whole person uses the faculty of understanding as a starting point or logical base upon which the other faculties rest.

The next two faculties, the imagination and the passions, are tied in closely with impressions. Through the power of imagination, for example, one conjures up vivid images which, in turn, produce strong feelings that go beyond correct judgments associated with the understanding. "The imagination of man," Hume asserts, "is naturally sublime, delighted with whatever is remote and extraordinary"; and with beauty and taste. It is the faculty, in sum, that has a compelling attraction for poets, priests, and politicians.[78]

In his description of the faculty of the passions, Hume was original and influential. Since he held that human motivation stems from man's emotional nature, he, as Locke had done earlier, argued that appeals to the passions of pleasure and pain are necessary to persuade the will to act. But he departed from Locke and the classical scholars in boldly claiming that "reason is and ought only to be the slave of the passions, and can never pretend to any other office than to serve and obey them."[79] At first glance, it appears difficult to reconcile this statement with Hume's career-long commitment to the use of soundly-conceived and well-executed arguments. Upon a closer examination, however, we may glimpse the true meaning of this startling observation. What he is trying to say, we believe after studying all of his major writings, is that the understanding and the passions must be in tune with each other. If a person is not emotionally committed to a course of action recommended by reason, the result will be ineffective in the long run. It is the purpose, therefore, of reason to serve the passions by guiding them toward a thoughtful conclusion.

Further evidence of Hume's concern in having the understanding and the passions to reinforce each other may be noted in the following excerpt taken from his *Enquiry*:

> Eloquence, when at its highest pitch, leaves little room for reason or reflection; but addressing itself entirely to the fancy or the affections, captivates the willing hearers, and subdues their understanding. Happily, this pitch it seldom attains.
>
> But what a Tully or a Demosthenes could scarcely effect over a Roman or Athenian audience, every Capuchian, every itinerant or stationary teacher can perform over the generality of mankind, and in a higher degree, by touching such gross and vulgar passions."[80]

The ultimate faculty of the mind is the will. It is this fourth element that must be stimulated if appropriate action is to take place. For this to occur, as Hume conceives it, a sequential, hierarchical pattern is helpful. First of all, the understanding receives logically-constructed arguments that meet the test of consistency with facts and with themselves.[81] Next these claims, which often begin as ideas, are transformed into impressions by the imagination; and as these strong impressions stir the passions, belief is generated.[82] It is at this juncture that persuasion of the will results.

The Principles of Association

Another major aspect of Hume's description of the nature of the mind that has important implications for rhetorical theory is his discussion of the principles of "connexion or association." This doctrine explains how thoughts are united together by three different, but related processes—resemblance, contiguity, and cause to effect. When we observe a particular object, event, or person, for instance, our mind is inclined to turn to its counterpart, which projects the image of being very similar. Hume illustrates this point with the following argument:

> We may . . . observe, as the first experiment of our present purpose, that upon the appearance of the picture of an absent friend, our idea of him is evidently enlivened by the *resemblance*, and that every passion which that idea occasions, whether of joy or sorrow, acquires new force and vigour. In producing this effect, there concur both a relation and a present impression. . . .[83]

As might be expected, the associative principle of resemblance, which gains its thrust from experience, helps the rhetor create arguments from analogy. Resemblance, in short, teaches us to recognize ideas and impressions that are "conjoined with each other."[84]

Hume uses the term "contiguity" to depict the second element of association. This concept refers to such ideas as geographical position in a sequential pattern or to the issue of time as it pertains to the moment an event occurred. If two points converge in a spatial sequence, thus rendering them adjacent, they are contiguous; as a result, a strong associative bond exists between them. Similarly if two related objects are present concurrently, there is a tendency for the mind to connect them.

The questions of time and space have a special significance when analyzing contiguity because, as Hume puts it, "distance diminishes the force of every idea." Consequently, the closer an object or an idea appears to us, the stronger the relationship will be. For this reason, the presence of an object is able to transport the mind to what is a connecting link or uniting bond with far greater vivacity and force than what is possible merely by thinking about it.[85]

Hume's discussion of the third element of association—cause and effect—was perhaps his most significant contribution to philosophical and rhetorical thought. Throughout the pages of the *Enquiry* he constantly affirms and reaffirms his views on causal relationships. He does so by defining what is meant by the terms, shows how they are a central part of the doctrine of association, and demonstrates the unique role that experience plays in establishing the reciprocal connection between cause and effect.

Cause is defined as "an object, followed by another, and where all the objects similar to the first are followed by objects similar to the second. . . ."[86] In other words, whenever we observe that B consistently follows the appearance of A, we may infer that A is the cause and B is the effect. This inference is made possible by the doctrine of association. For what it suggests is that our mind has made a connection between A and B in such a way that "they become proofs of each other's existence. . . ."[87] A typical example of how this causal relationship operates, Hume notes, may be seen when our mind focuses on a wound (Object A) that we have received. This reflection immediately stimulates our senses thereby reminding us of the pain (Object B) that accompanied the wound.

Hume makes it clear that we cannot determine causal relationships by relying on *a priori* reasoning. Such knowledge can only be learned through experience based on repeated observations. This method of analysis, which is the centerpiece of his experimental theory, is the principal means of enabling us to evaluate all matters of fact. [88] How, for instance, do we come to know that a dry piece of wood thrown into a fire will strengthen rather than extinguish a flame? We know this, Hume points out, by recalling similar incidents throughout our lifetime.

Hume's experimental probes into the nature of the mind, as the preceding discussion demonstrates, prompted him to deal with such topics as ideas and impressions; the four faculties—understanding, imagination, passions, and the will; and the concept of cause and effect. It is also of importance to note, as we conclude this section, that he viewed the mind as a bundle of sensory perceptions held together by association, and that a belief may be defined as "a lively idea related to or associated with a present impression."[89] It remains now for us to see how these explanations of the nature of the mind form the basis for creating a theory of reasoning.

The Two Types of Reasoning

Hume used the terms "demonstrative" and "moral" to identify the two kinds of reasoning that result from the nature of the mind. The major difference between these argumentative approaches, as we shall now see, is the degree of certainty inherent in the claims.

Demonstrative Reasoning

This form of reasoning emphasizes the "relations of ideas," and premises that are "either intuitively or demonstratively certain. . . ."[90] It typifies the reasoning process associated with the mathematical sciences, including arithmetic, algebra, and geometry. Of this type of high level reasoning, Hume says "that the ideas . . . being sensible, are always clear and determinate, the smallest distinction between them is immediately perceptible, and the same terms are still expressive of the same ideas, without ambiguity or variation. . . ."[91] Since demonstrative reasoning leads us to claims that are certain, they cannot be disputed; thus they are outside of the field of rhetoric, which is incapable of rising above the level of probability. This, then, is the rationale for Hume's introduction of his theory of moral reasoning.

Moral Reasoning

This is the designation that Hume uses to explain the kind of reasoning that takes place in human affairs. To him, moral reasoning is the principal source of our knowledge and the moving force responsible for our behavior and actions.[92] Its subject matter consists of factual data—particularly cause to effect relationships—related to existence. If a speech or written treatise does not utilize abstract reasoning concerning "quantity or number," he argues, it fails to fulfill its duty to enlighten us on matters of fact or existence. When this is the case, the work contains "nothing but sophistry and illusion" and should, therefore, be cast into the "flames."[93]

The four elements of moral reasoning are experience, testimony, analogy, and calculation of probabilities. The most important of these, according to Hume, is experience because of its powerful influence on the other three. As we observed in our treatment of the doctrine of association, it is experience that informs us of the relation between cause and effect and "enables us to infer the existence of one object from that of another."[94] Moreover, it is experience that guides our reasoning on all issues involving particular facts. With these firmly-held beliefs etched in his mind, Hume felt justified in asserting that "a uniform experience amounts to a proof. . . ."[95] By the same token, however, experience may be used to show how an adversary's claim, which runs counter to custom, must be rejected because of its deviation from known facts.

A by-product of experience is testimony, which constitutes a second significant element of moral reasoning. This pervasive form of evidence, based on the accounts of expert or lay witnesses, is always grounded in experience. Hume lists five criteria for evaluating the worth of testimony. These tests may be phrased in the following interrogatory form:

1. Are there a sufficient number of witnesses?
2. Is the testimony offset by contrary testimony?
3. Do the witnesses have a strong character?
4. Do the witnesses "have an interest in what they affirm?"
5. Is the testimony presented in a manner free from hesitation and from "too violent asservations?"[96]

If the testimony does not meet all of the above criteria, it falls short of the probability needed to convince a thoughtful listener or reader.

Arguments from analogy, like those from testimony, are drawn from experience. Consequently, personal observations made throughout one's career have instilled in that individual knowledge of the associative quality of resemblance, making it possible to see connections between two objects or events. If the relationships we perceive between two ideas or things conform to known reality, the analogical argument we construct in this instance should be persuasive. But Hume recommends that we take special care not to overstate a perceived similarity. "Nothing so like eggs," he asserts; "yet no one, on account of this appearing similarity, expects the same taste and relish in all of them."[97]

The last element of moral reasoning is called "calculation of probabilities." Hume divides this discussion of this point into two categories: (1) "probability of chances" and (2) "probability of causes." We measure the effectiveness of a probability of chance by contrasting the possibilities on one side with those on another. By weighing the numerical strength of each position, we may determine which side contains the higher degree of probability.

The same procedure is followed when assessing the probability of causes. Again we weigh the experimental findings in support of each case, and act in accordance with the superior evidence. The following excerpt should prove helpful in seeing how the notion of calculation of probabilities is an important rhetorical strategy in moral reasoning:

> A wise man . . . proportions his belief to the evidence. In such conclusions as are founded on infallible experience, he expects the event with the last degree of assurance, and regards his past experience as full proof of the existence of that event. In other cases, he proceeds with more caution: he weighs the opposite experiments; he considers which side is supported by the greater number

of experiments; to that side he inclines, with doubt and hesitation; and when at last he fixes his judgement, the evidence exceeds not what we properly call *probability*. All probability, then, supposes an opposition of experiments and observations, where the one side is found to over balance the other, and to produce, a degree of evidence, proportioned to the superiority. . . ."[98]

By stressing the significance of the use of statistical-based probability as an essential part of the decision-making process, Hume, it would appear, laid the foundation for an important dimension of modem experimental methodology.

The last point to be considered in examining Hume's philosophy of moral reasoning is to see how it makes use of audience analysis and adaptation. What we will find later on is that his ideas on adapting discourse to its end, and to an audience were to have a profound influence both on his contemporary Campbell and on the twentieth-century scholar Chaim Perelman.

Audience Analysis and Adaptation

Since the audience, in Hume's opinion, is the primary focal point in the initiation of discourse, it is necessary for the rhetor to anticipate from the outset how his or her appeal will be received. To succeed in this endeavor, appropriate responses must be given to these two questions:

1. Is the discourse, as it relates to the discipline or field of study under consideration, adapted to its end?
2. Is it adapted to the nature of the audience?

Hume's theory of moral reasoning will provide answers to these queries.

Adapting Discourse to Its End

Each discipline or field of study, Hume tells us, has a specific purpose that should be achieved. Adhering to the teachings of Cicero, he noted that history, for example, has as its goal "to instruct"; poetry seeks to please; and eloquence, or oratory, is designed to persuade. To implement their ends, history is concerned with the faculty of understanding; poetry with the imagination and the passions; and eloquence with all four faculties, beginning with the understanding and proceeding in order to the imagination, the passions, and the will. Hume gives this advice to a critic who wishes to ascertain whether or not a rhetor has succeeded in reaching his or her goal: "These ends we must carry constantly in our view when we peruse any performance, and we must be able to judge how far the means employed are adapted to their respective purposes. . . ."[99]

Adapting to the Nature of the Audience

The two types of hearers or readers who captured the interest of Hume were the particular and the philosophical audience. A particular audience consists of men and women who not only share the general traits of human nature but those characteristics peculiar to the specific group of people who have assembled to receive a message. The author of an address, for instance, knows in advance that the hearers consist of human beings who have four faculties of the mind; the knowledge to distinguish the feelings produced by ideas and by impressions; and the ability to make associations with respect to objects and events through the power of resemblance, contiguity, and cause-to-effect connections. The author is also aware that all people have a sense of taste, even though "few are qualified to give judgment on any work of art or establish their own sentiment as the standard of beauty. . . ."[100] Further, the rhetor can know that people as a whole are dogmatic beings who are inclined to affirm their own positions and to reject outright all counter arguments regardless of their merit.[101]

From these considerations of a person in general, the rhetor or the critic must next focus on the composition of the particular auditors. This would include an analysis of such points as their educational and cultural background, their geographical locale, their religious affiliation, their occupational status, the question of time when they assembled, and their strongly-held beliefs. An orator whose duty it is to persuade, Hume points out, is constrained to adapt the message to the listeners' "genius, interests, opinions, passions, and prejudices. . . ."[102]

In emphasizing the above points, Hume offers two suggestions for helping the rhetor or the critic to adapt to a particular audience. First, he notes that if the auditors are biased toward the speaker, it will be necessary to break down the hostility by using conciliatory appeals in the introduction.[103] Secondly, he advises the critic whose purpose is to evaluate an address delivered in an earlier historical period not to rely wholly on the standards of taste that are operative at the time the critique is written. Rather the critic should seek to place himself or herself in the audience that heard the presentation firsthand. In this way the perceptions would have a greater degree of accuracy and relevance.[104]

Hume's discussion of a particular audience had its roots in the works of numerous previous authors. Notwithstanding this fact, the phrasing of his ideas, as observed here, was fresh and influential because of the way it was integrated into his principles of moral reasoning.

As he turned to an analysis of the second kind of audience—the philosophical, Hume showed a greater degree of originality. For us to be a member of this ideal audience, he felt, is to strive for "a proper impartiality in our judgments," to free ourselves from all prejudices, and to show a capacity for comprehending the speaker's arguments. These high standards, he asserts in one of his written dialogues, could not be met by an Athenian mob. They could, however, be fulfilled by those who have a strong philosophical nature and training. When addressing this thoughtful audience, Hume suggests that we follow these guidelines:

> To begin with clear and self-evident principles, to advance by timorous and sure steps, to review frequently our conclusions and examine accurately all their consequences . . . are the only methods, by which we can ever hope to reach the truth, and attain a proper stability in our determinations. . . .[105]

Although the philosophical audience, with its seemingly excessive reliance on idealism, may be outside the scope of typical discourse presentations, it is, as we shall see in the final section of this volume, strikingly consistent with Perelman's notion of the universal audience and with Jurgen Habermas' views on the "ideal speaking situation."

Hume, we may conclude, contributed vitally to the evolution of rhetorical thought. More than any other British epistemologist, he taught us the value of experience as a source of knowledge; and of using moral reasoning rather than syllogistic arguments to buttress our claims. In short, he has revealed to us forcefully that rhetoric is not only a humane field of study, but is a major part of the social science tradition as well.

David Hartley

The conclusions reached by the physician David Hartley in his *Observations on Man, His Frame, His Duty, and His Expectations,* published in 1749—ten years after *The Treatise on Human Nature*—are strikingly similar to those set forth by Hume. Although he makes no reference to Hume's works, Hartley doubtless is indebted to them. Throughout his volume he draws upon general classical rhetorical principles and upon Locke, seeking "to do for human nature what Newton did for the solar system."[106] Thus the doctrine of association, which was the basic element in Hartley's theory of knowledge, is as fundamental to man's intellectual nature as gravitation is to the planets. All ideas, he argued, are derived from sensations caused by vibrations in the nerves of the muscles. As ideas in their elementary form enter the mind they are gradually transformed through the power of association into complex beliefs and attitudes that stimulate human action.

An essential aspect of Hartley's system is the view that all developments in life, including persuasive communication events, "are links in an eternal chain of cause and effects."[107] The subject of pleasure and pain illustrates how causal relationships are a part of one's daily life. From the basic starting point of sensation six other pleasures and pains are generated, each dependent upon those that precede it. The seven classes and the order in which they occur are sensation, imagination, ambition, self-interest, sympathy, theopathy, (i.e. religious emotion), and moral sense.

In formulating his psychological and moral theories, Hartley, unlike Vico and Hume, rarely alluded to specific rhetoricians or their works. Yet his debt to classical rhetorical precepts is unmistakable. When analyzing propositions and the nature of assent, he urged that a plain didactic style should be used to appeal to the understanding, and figurative language to stimulate the passions.[108] More importantly he recognized the role of rhetoric in producing the pleasures and pains of imagination. Convinced that rhetoric like history conforms to reality, he defined invention as "the art of producing new Beauties in Works of Imagination, and new Truths in Matters of Science."[109] To describe how the communicator stirs the imagination, Hartley turned to traditional rhetorical doctrines. He advocated an inventive process characterized by forceful logical, emotional, and ethical appeals. Further he recommended that these available means of persuasion should be properly arranged and expressed in moving language designed to excite the passions. Out of such an approach human conduct is altered.[110]

In still another important respect Hartley found a helpful ally in rhetoric. More than most of his contemporaries, he used classical persuasive strategies to outline his book and to argue his thesis. Employing many of the Aristotelian and Ciceronian elements of logos, he attempted to show, for example, the relevancy and reliability of Christianity. Repeatedly he relied upon cause to effect reasoning, the argument from sign, and indirect testimony. Additionally he incorporated refutation in his discussion in an effort to demonstrate the good consequences of Christian piety. It would appear, then, that Hartley's elaborate system of associational psychology, which was to have a noticeable impact on Campbell and Priestley as well as on nineteenth-century writers, used traditional rhetorical theory and modem epistemological thought as important sources.

Lord Kames

The attempts of Hume and Hartley to produce a philosophy of human nature based upon classical theories and modem science gave a new dimension to psychological and sociological thought, and created a challenge for literary critics to employ a similar method. One of the leading proponents of this approach was Henry Home [Lord Kames] whose efforts contributed to the "Age of Reason" in Scottish literature. That Kames was influenced by experimental methodology is observable in his rigid adherence to the Newtonian theory and to Locke's doctrine of the association of ideas. In his work *Elements of Criticism*, published in 1762, Kames combines the analytical and synthetic methods. He begins with effects and by tracing a series of particular causes, reaches a general concept. From here he descends slowly, explaining consequences by the universal law which he has established.

Kames was especially intrigued with Locke's principle of connections; that is, "perceptions and ideas in a train." There is, he believed, a definite connection of ideas in one's mind. "It is required [in every work of art]," said Kames, "that, like an organic system, its parts be orderly arranged and mutually connected, bearing each of them a relation to the whole."[111] Working from this premise, Kames found fault with many of the ancients. Homer, Pindar, Horace, and Virgil are criticized for not observing the rules of connection, order, and arrangement."[112] He likewise was one of the first writers to fault Aristotle's *Poetics*. He agreed with Aristotle on the unity of action, but thought he put too much emphasis on the unities of time and place. On this point, he said, "we are under no necessity to copy the ancients; and our critics are guilty of mistake, in admitting no greater latitude of place and time than was admitted in Greece and Rome."[113]

Kames was willing to endorse any of the ancient teachings which were based on reason. He found it easy, therefore, to praise Aristotle's doctrine of tragedy because it "depends upon natural operations of the human mind."[114] But Kames was quick to condemn an unwarranted imitation of the classics. In all, Kames' wide-ranging scholarship, his openness to new ideas, and his leadership capacity, made him a favorite in Edinburgh society and a literary model to be emulated by such men as Adam Smith, Hugh Blair, and James Boswell.

Joseph Priestley

Like many earlier epistemologists who turned their attention to rhetoric, Joseph Priestley was a man of many interests and accomplishments. He was a Unitarian preacher and theologian, as well as an educator. Most of all he was a renowned scientist who discovered oxygen and invented soda water. His major contribution to the rhetoric of Western thought was his

Course of Lectures on Oratory and Criticism.[115] Published in 1777, this volume contains many of the benchmarks of belletristic rhetoric. In its basic thrust, however, it more correctly belongs to the epistemological school of thought. At least this was Priestley's intention, agreeing to put his lectures in print only after he had convinced himself that he would be the first author to apply Hartley's principles of association to the field of oratory and criticism. That he fulfilled his promise of relating Hartley's teachings to rhetoric cannot be denied. Even when Priestley is giving the appearance of subscribing to Aristotle's treatment of topics, he is actually superimposing upon them Hartley's doctrine of association. Topics and ideas, he argues, are tied in with experience and recollection which, in turn, are "associated by means of their connection with, and relation to one another."[116]

Hartley is again the source for Priestley's discussion of style and taste. After acknowledging that pleasure derived from a discourse results from a stimulation of the imagination and passions, he rejects the popular interpretation that those "delicate sensations" and "sensible feelings" experienced by the listener or reader are "reflex, or internal senses."[117] Priestley explains his own position as follows:

> According to Dr. Hartley's theory, those sensations consist of nothing more than a congeries or combination of ideas and sensations, separately indistinguishable, but which were formerly associated either with the idea itself that excites them, or with some other idea, or circumstance, attending the introduction of them. It is this latter hypothesis that I adopt, and, by the help of it, I hope to be able to throw some new light on this curious subject.[118]

In a subsequent lecture on imagination and taste, Priestley likewise alludes to Hartley to explain how the pleasures that are received from a "country landscape," a "rural scene," or a "romance" come from the mental principles of association.[119]

The *Lectures on Oratory and Criticism,* it should be pointed out, are more than a practical application of Hartley's psychology. Indeed, the study is so dependent upon other seventeenth and eighteenth century works such as Locke's *Essay Concerning Human Understanding,* Hume's *Enquiry into the Principles of Morals,* Kames' *Elements of Criticism,* and John Ward's *Systems of Oratory* that Priestley has been called "more an 'index scholar' in rhetoric than an original thinker."[120] It is of interest to note, however, that the two critics who made this assessment also observed that Priestley's "psychological reinterpretation of traditional rhetorical principles in terms of associational psychology" gives him a permanent place in the history of Western rhetorical thought.[121]

Summary

What we have seen in the foregoing discussion are major contributions to rhetorical thought made by a group of epistemologists who achieved fame in a wide variety of scholarly areas. Well versed in psychology, philosophy, and science, they drew ideas from their field of special knowledge, and applied them to theories of human communication. In doing so, they profoundly influenced George Campbell and Richard Whately, the writings of whom will constitute our principal focus in the next chapter.

Notes

1 Hugh C. Dick, ed., *Selected Writings of Francis Bacon* (New York: The Modern Library, 1955), p. X.

2 Karl Wallace has observed that the "central pillars" of the *Advancement of Learning* "are the psychological faculties." *Francis Bacon on the Nature of Man* (Urbana, Ill: University of Illinois Press, 1967), p. 2.

3 *Selected Writings of Francis Bacon*, p. 230.

4 *Ibid.*, p. 309.

5 Francis Bacon, "Advancement of Learning," in *The Works of Lord Bacon*, 2 vols. (London, Bohn, 1871), I, p. 48.

6 *Ibid.*, p. 254.

7 *Ibid.*, p. 255.

8 Karl R. Wallace, *Francis Bacon on Communication & Rhetoric* (Chapel Hill, N.C., 1943), p. 66.

9 *Ibid.*, p. 71.

10 *Ibid.*, p. 73.

11 *The Works of Lord Bacon*, 1, p. 310.

12 *Ibid.*, pp. 315, 319.

13 *Francis Bacon on Communication & Rhetoric*, p. 78.

14 *Ibid.*, p. 81. Also see pp. 82–83.

15 "Novum organum," in *ibid.*, p. 465.

16 See *ibid.*, pp. 469–487.

17 *Ibid.*, p. 470.

18 *Ibid.*

19 *Ibid.*

20 *Ibid.*, p. 471.

21 *Ibid.*, p. 487.

22 "The Great Instauration," in *ibid.*, pp. 441–42.

23 Dick makes this claim in the introduction of *ibid.*, XVII.

24 Thomas Sprat, *History of the Royal Society*, Jackson I. Cope and Harold W. Jones, eds. (St. Louis: Washington University Press, 1959), p. 35.

25 René Descartes, *A Discourse on Method* (London: J. M. Dent and Sons, 1941), p. 7.

26 *Ibid.*, p. 15.

27 *Ibid.*, p. 7.

28 *Ibid.*, pp. 15–17.

29 *Ibid.*, p. 50.

30 This conclusion appears in the editor's commentary in the introduction of *Discourse on Method*, XI.

31 Wilbur S. Howell, *Logic and Rhetoric in England, 1500–1700* (New York: Russell & Russell, Inc., 1961), pp. 346–49.

32 *Discourse on Method*, XI.

33 Cited in Howell, *Logic and Rhetoric in England*, p. 343.

34 Hugh Davidson, *Audience, Words, and Art: Studies in Seventeenth-Century French Rhetoric* (Columbus, Ohio: The Ohio State University Press, 1965), p. 82.

35 John Locke, *An Essay Concerning Human Understanding*, 2 vols. (London: D. Browne, et al, 1760), II, p. 106.

36 *Ibid.*, I, p. 192.

37 *Ibid.*, p. 367.

38 *Ibid.*, II, pp. 290–99.

39 *Ibid.*, I, pp. 203–210.

40 Leon Festinger, *A Theory of Cognitive Dissonance* (New York: Row, Peterson, 1957).

41 Vico was born in 1670 and died in 1744. In honor of the tercentenary year of his birth, the following comprehensive volume was published: Giorgi Tagliacozzo and Hayden White, eds., *Giambattista Vico: An International Symposium* (Baltimore: The Johns Hopkins Press, 1969).

42 The most famous of these lectures was presented in 1708 under the title *De nostri temporis studiorum ratione.* It was first published in English with the title: "On the Study Methods of our Time." See Elio Granturco, ed., Giambattista Vico, *On the Study Methods of our Time* (Indianapolis: Bobbs Merrill, 1965).

43 Max H. Fisch and Thomas G. Bergen, eds., *The Autobiography of Giambattista Vico* (Urica, N.Y.: Great Seal Books, 1963), p. 120.

44 *Ibid.*, p. 138.

45 Thomas G. Bergin and Max H. Fisch, eds., *The New Science of Giambattista Vico* (Ithaca, N.Y.: Cornell University Press, 1958), pp. 65, 755–76.

46 Grassi has observed: "The thinker who tried, at the end of the humanistic tradition, to overcome the dualism of *pathos and logos* . . . was Vico; and the basis

of his effort was a discussion of the preeminence of topical versus critical philosophy." Ernesto Grassi, "Critical Philosophy or Topical Philosophy?" in *Giambattista Vico: An International Symposium*, pp. 41–42.

47 This is a major premise in *On the Study Methods of our Time*. For an instructive criticism, see Grassi's essay.

48 Alfonsina A. Grimaldi, *The Universal Humanity of Giambattista Vico* (New York: S. F. Vanni, 1958), p. 52.

49 *Ibid.*

50 *Ibid.*, p. 53.

51 *Autobiography*, p. 139. In addition to Plato, Tacitus, and Bacon, Vico selected Grotius as one of his four favorite authors. See Enrico De Mas, "Vico's Four Authors," in *Vico: An International Symposium*, pp. 3–14.

52 Grimaldi, p. 3.

53 *The New Science*, XXXIII.

54 *Ibid.*, p. 104.

55 Isaiah Berlin, "One of the Boldest Innovators of the History of Human Thought," *The New York Times Magazine*, November 23, 1969.

56 *The New Science*, pp. 104–105.

57 *Ibid.*, p. 104.

58 René Wellek, "The Supposed Influence of Vico on England and Scotland in the Eighteenth Century," in *Vico: An International Symposium*. pp. 215–23.

59 *The New York Times Magazine*, November 23, 1969.

60 J. H. Plumb, "Reason and Unreason in the Eighteenth Century," Unpublished address delivered at Ohio State University, April 9, 1969.

61 *Ibid.*

62 For an analysis of Blair's preaching techniques, see James L. Golden, "Hugh Blair: Minister of St. Giles," *Quarterly Journal of Speech*, 38 (April, 1952), 155–60.

63 *Ibid.*

64 Samuel Miller, *A Brief Retrospect of the Eighteenth Century*, 2 vols. (New York: T. and J. Swords, 1803), II, p. 425; and Hugo Arnot, *History of Edinburgh* (Edinburgh: T. Turnbull, 1818), pp. 516, 567.

65 "Reason and Unreason in the Eighteenth Century in England."

66 V. C. Chappell, ed., *The Philosophy of David Hume* (New York: The Modern Library, 1963), VII.

67 James Golden and Douglas Ehninger, "The Extrinsic Sources of Blair's Popularity," *Southern Speech Journal*, 22 (Fall, 1956), 28.

68 Michael Joyce, *Edinburgh: The Golden Age* (London: Longmans, Green, 1951), pp. 1, 6.

69 John Hill Burton, *Life and Correspondence of David Hume* (Edinburgh: W. Tait, 1846), II, p. 229.

70 J. Y. T Greig, *David Hume* (New York: Oxford University Press, 1931), p. 59.

71 David Hume to Henry Home, June 13, 1742, in John Burton, pp. 144–45.

72 The quotation was drawn from *De Oratore*, II, LXXXIV pp. 343–44. Greig criticized Hume for relying too heavily upon Cicero's *De Natura Deorum* when writing his *Dialogues*. Greig, *David Hume*, p. 231.

73 L. A. Selby-Bigge, ed., *Enquiries Concerning the Human Understanding* and *Concerning the Principles of Morals by David Hume* (Oxford: The Clarendon Press, 1936), p. 7.

74 It is important to note that the term "philosophy" in the eighteenth century was used to cover a broad range of disciplines including psychology.

75 *An Enquiry Concerning Human Understanding* (Buffalo, N.Y.: Prometheus Books, 1988), p. 21.

76 *Ibid.*, p. 24.

77 *Ibid.*, p. 59.

78 *Ibid.*, pp. 57 and 146.

79 *A Treatise of Human Nature*, ed. By T. H. Green and T. H. Grose, 2 vols. (New York: Longmans, Green, and Co., 1898), II, p. 195.

80 *An Enquiry Concerning Human Understanding*, pp. 107–108.

81 *Ibid.*, p. 88.

82 Although this may be the usual pattern, Hume states in his *Treatise of Human Nature* that a belief may come first and then proceed to influence the imagination and the passions. See Mossner edition, Penguin Books, New York, 1984, pp. 169–170.

83 *An Enquiry Concerning Human Understanding*, p. 50.

84 *Ibid.*, p. 134.

85 *Ibid.*, p. 51.

86 *Ibid.*, p. 72.

87 *Ibid.*, p. 71.

88 On this point, Hume asserts: "All reasonings concerning matter of fact seem to be founded on the relation of cause and effect." *Ibid.*, p. 29.

89 *A Treatise of Human Nature*, I, p. 396.

90 *An Enquiry Concerning Human Understanding*, pp. 28 and 36.

91 *Ibid.*, p. 58.

92 *Ibid.*, p. 148.

93 *Ibid.*, p. 149.

94 *Ibid.*, p. 148.

95 *Ibid.*, p. 106.

96 *Ibid.*, p. 103.

97 *Ibid.*, p. 101.

98 *Ibid.*

99 "Of the Standard of Taste," in V. C. Chappell, ed.; *The Philosophy of David Hume* (New York: The Modern Library, 1963), p. 494.

100 *Ibid.*

101 *An Enquiry Concerning Human Understanding*, p. 145.

102 "Of the Standard of Taste," p. 492.

103 *Ibid.*

104 *Ibid.*

105 *An Enquiry Concerning Human Understanding*, p. 136.

106 Leslie Stephen, *History of English Thought in the Eighteenth Century*, 2 vols. (London: G. P. Putnam's Sons, 1876), II, p. 66.

107 *Ibid.*, p. 64.

108 David Hartley, *Observations on Man, His Frame, His Duty, and His Expectations* (1749) (Gainesville, Fla., 1966), p. 357.

109 *Ibid.*, p. 434.

110 *Ibid.*, p. 432.

111 Henry Lord Kames Home, *Elements of Criticism*, ed. by Abraham Mills (New York: Huntington & Savage, 1849), p. 23.

112 *Ibid.*, pp. 23–24.

113 See the discussion on "The Three Unities," in *ibid.*, pp. 429–440. In particular, observe p. 432.

114 See chapter on "Three Unities."

115 Vincent Bevilacqua and Richard Murphy. eds. *A Course of Lectures on Oratory and Criticism by Joseph Priestley* (Carbondale, Ill.: Southern Illinois University Press, 1965).

116 *Ibid.*, p. 22.

117 *Ibid.*, p. 72.

118 *Ibid.*, pp. 72–73.

119 *Ibid.*, p. 130.

120 *Ibid.*, p. 111.

121 *Ibid.*

SECTION NINE:
ENLIGHTENMENT RHETORICS

Section Nine
Enlightenment Rhetorics

James Herrick

All that can possibly be required of Language, is, to convey our ideas clearly to the minds of others, and, at the same time, in such a dress, as by pleasing and interesting them, shall most effectually strengthen the impressions which we seek to make.

—Hugh Blair

It is customary to locate the beginning of the "modern" age somewhere in the late seventeenth or early eighteenth century, the period known as the Enlightenment. If modernity involves questioning the received truths of Christian tradition, elevating rationality over other sources of truth, such as authority, seeking solutions to social problems by means of scientific method, and viewing the universe as governed by inviolable physical laws, then perhaps the intellectual developments in Europe in the late seventeenth and throughout the eighteenth centuries do mark a major transition in Western thought.

Several writers were particularly important in bringing about some of the changes that have traditionally been employed as markers of the modern period. Isaac Newton (1642–1727) described physical laws governing the universe in his *Principia Mathematica* (1687). John Locke (1632–1704) suggested an empirical basis of human knowing in his *Essay Concerning Human Understanding* (1690). David Hume's *Enquiry Concerning Human Understanding* (1748) explored the rational operations of the human mind. Jean-Jacques Rousseau (1712–1778) outlined a theory of government centered on the individual citizen in *The Social Contract* (1762). Francois Voltaire (1694–1778) subjected the bases of Christian belief to severe criticism in his *Dictionairre Philosophique* (1764) and several other works.

This chapter examines some developments in rhetorical theory during the eighteenth century, first on the European Continent, and then in Britain. The legacy of Renaissance Humanism is evident in writers like Giovanni Battista Vico in Italy. We will consider Vico's surprisingly modern theory of the rhetorical evolution of the human mind. Following our exploration of Vico, we will move from the European Continent to the British Isles to examine a variety of rhetorical theories that speculate about matters as disparate as psychology, argument, preaching, style, the beneficial use of leisure time, and even correcting a telltale Irish accent.

It has been noted by some scholars that the eighteenth century marks a period in which rhetorical theory turned away from its traditional concern for the invention of arguments, and toward aesthetic matters of style and good delivery. One leading expert on the period, Barbara Warnick, suggests that this shift in emphasis reflects the influence of Ramus in the sixteenth century and Descartes in the seventeenth. Both writers moved argument and proof out of the domain of rhetoric and into the domains of logic, dialectic, and mathematics. Warnick writes, "by the late seventeenth century, rhetorical logic had been displaced...." The result was the emergence of what Warnick calls a "managerial" emphasis in rhetorical studies. "During the Enlightenment, French and Scottish rhetorics turned to a managerial view of rhetoric that distinguished the discovery of knowledge through reasoning from communication of content to others." That is, in earlier periods, rhetoric had performed both functions—discovery and communication of knowledge. Eighteenth century writers often seem content to allow rhetoric only the latter responsibility. Warnick identifies a corresponding shift from rhetoric as guiding the *production* of discourse, to rhetoric as enhancing the *consumption* of discourse. "While concern for invention and the production of discourse receded, intense interest in the problem of receptive competence emerged to take its place."

Though it would be an exaggeration to say that invention is completely excluded from rhetoric in eighteenth- and early nineteenth-century rhetorics, the truth of Warnick's observation often is born out in the rhetorical scholarship of this period. In the discussions that follow, note the emphasis on matters such as style, taste, delivery, and the imagination, as contrasted to earlier emphasis in rhetorical scholarship on arguments, proofs, invention, and reason. At the same time, we might also note in this period a shift from an earlier concern for rhetoric's public role as the *techne* of civil discourse and community business to a more private interest in rhetoric as a window on the human mind or a means of personal refinement.

VICO ON RHETORIC AND HUMAN THOUGHT

Among the later writers in the Italian Humanist tradition, the most important is Giambattista Vico. Vico was an Italian philosopher born in Naples in 1668. Vico's father was a bookseller, and he spent a great deal of time reading as a youth. Lawyers held a prominent place in the Naples of the late seventeenth century, and Vico studied originally for a career in law. However, his interests eventually turned toward literature, history, mathematics, philosophy, and rhetoric. Something of a recluse, Vico spent long hours alone teaching himself philosophy, law, and literature. He was particularly drawn to the logical works of Peter of Spain, the speculative theology of John Duns Scotus, and the political theories and metaphysics of the Spanish writer, Francisco Suarez. Vico studied Plato, and was intrigued with the Neoplatonism of his Renaissance predecessors, Pico and Ficino.

Vico versus Descartes

Vico wrote passionately in response to the great philosopher and mathematician René Descartes, who despised rhetoric and wished to relegate it to an obscure place in the academy. In works such as *On the Study Methods of Our Time* (1708), Vico argued that the mathematical proofs of Descartes were just as reliant on symbols as were the orations of the rhetoricians. In other words, mathematics was not somehow founded on transcendent, necessary, and unchanging truths. Nevertheless, the idea that science would provide a rational basis for future societies was gaining influence, and Vico sought to answer what he viewed as a dangerous cultural development.

The study, and especially the practice, of rhetoric provided the only antidote to the broadening influence of scientific rationalism. Vico argued that rhetoric, not reason, was the basis of social life, and that the growing hegemony of scientific thinking threatened to undermine the common beliefs and values—the *sensus communis*—that provide the basis for society. Speech, especially poetic speech, provides the foundation of civilized society, not philosophical or scientific reason.

Vico's fear of the dominance of science, with its emphasis on individual reason as opposed to the common sense of the community, cannot be overstated. Descartes was his *bête noire,* and he argued strenuously that only the constructive and communal use of rhetoric provided the means of opposing the corrosive effects of the individual and sceptical use of reason advocated by Descartes.

The Rhetoric of the Imagination

Though he greatly admired the philosophy of Descartes, Vico sought answers about the nature of human thought in two unusual places—poetry and mythology. This odd approach placed him beyond the pale of Neapolitan intellectual life. Vico was seen as an eccentric and a dreamer, and his thinking was "dismissed as obscure, speculative, and unsound (*stravagante,* as the Italians put it), or even slightly mad." Vico inherited much from the Italian Humanists, in whose wisdom he was schooled, but he lived too late to be considered a Renaissance figure. Though he lived during the early Enlightenment, "he was not a typical man of the Enlightenment, looking down on earlier ages as times of 'darkness' and irrationality." Vico was as original in his thought as he is difficult to classify historically.

In 1697 Vico became a professor of rhetoric at Naples, a position he held for forty years. A poet himself, he held that "primitive men were necessarily poets because they possessed strong imaginations which compensated for the weakness of their reason." Vico argued that language originated with rhetorical devices native to the human imagination, and maintained that language allowed people to impose order on their existence, to create meaning out of meaninglessness, and to establish society. Vico's philosophy, then, focused on human history rather than on metaphysics. As Ernesto Grassi points out, for Vico "the problems that concern human beings—and these are the only kinds that can have scientific interest—are the ones that urge themselves upon us in the construction of the human world and therefore concern the realization of man as such."

Pursuing this interest in human history, Vico argued in works such as his *New Science* (1725) that historical method could be just as exact as mathematics. In advancing this thesis, Vico was opposing the views of Descartes, who had affirmed that the only certain knowledge was that which could not be doubted. Decisions in public life, Vico noted, were not usually based on certainties, but rather on careful weighing of options guided by prudence, or practical judgment. Vico was drawn, then, to Cicero's notion of the *perfectus orator,* or, as Michael Mooney summarizes the concept, "the 'finished orator' as a public servant whose ability with words is informed by a command of the whole cycle of learning." Such a person, guided by the union of wisdom and eloquence, could provide practical and moral leadership to the society. The orator became a heroic figure, one who spoke or wrote wisely and eloquently for the benefit of the whole society. The common good was predominant in humanist thinking, and the skilled orator had greater potential for contributing to that common good than did any other citizen.

Vico held that rhetoric was essential to all of the arts and all human ways of making sense of the world. By means of language, humans have imposed order on a fundamentally disordered nature. The "humanization of nature" takes place, not through rational or inferential thought, but rather through *ingenium,* or the innate human capacity to grasp similarities or relationships. The person of practical judgment must be able to "find analogies between matters that lie far apart and are apparently unrelated...." Grassi writes, "insight into relationships is not possible through a process of inference, but rather only through an original *in*-sight as invention and discovery (*inventio*)."

Vico held that this innate human capacity for recognizing or grasping similarities among different objects was central to the poetic or metaphoric nature of thought. Analogic thinking allowed insights that were crucial to the ordering and humanizing of the world. Discovering "connections, and so advancing the cause of civil life, is the proper work of ingenuity [*ingenium*]." Through the exercise of *ingenium,* "we surpass what lies before us in our sensory awareness." And, in the act of transcending perception, we become human. The language of metaphor and poetry "is the language that constitutes humanity."

Rhetoric and the Evolution of Human Thought

Thinking based on *ingenium* is more poetic than logical, more intuitive than rational, and arrives at insights rather than deductions. Such thinking is therefore actually productive of new knowledge, and not merely of reformulations of things already known. Vico, as we have noted, found direction for the development of this theory in Cicero and the rhetorical tradition rather than in the philosophers and logicians of the seventeenth and eighteenth centuries. Descartes, Vico thought, had ignored the vital rhetorical element in human thinking by focusing his attention solely on the method of demonstrable proof that moved by deduction from first principles to necessary conclusions.

Like other rhetorical theorists, Vico recognized the need for education in the arts of practical decision making about matters that did not yield to scientific analysis, issues like law, art, ethics, and politics. Human social life is lived in public space where most decisions are "contingent" or subject to various resolutions. Deductive logic is of limited use for such moral decision making, while rhetoric with its more flexible and practical characteristics, is essential.

Vico was "fascinated by the processes through which the human mind learns." In an effort to understand these processes, he advanced an intriguing theory of the relationship among language, thought, and experience based on four tropes, or rhetorical devices. Mooney explains the problem with which Vico started in developing this theory: "Given the richness of nature, every language lacks words to make note of certain items of experience." Thus, existing words must be imaginatively employed to allow both new modes of thinking and a broader range of expression. Tropes developed to make up for the lack of capacity in words alone. Thus, the first people "proceeded to create their world through the faculty of imagination rather than by pure abstract thought." As Katherine Gilbert and Helmut Kuhn express the concept, "the poet's imagination is the natural expression of humanity's childhood." It will be helpful to examine this intriguing concept in greater detail.

Vico was fascinated with early human cultures, and speculated about the evolution of language and human thought. His theory of the development of thought has been called "incomparably richer and more fully developed" than those advanced by other scholars of his generation. Vico posited that during "the childhood of the world," human thinking developed first by metaphor, or a comparison of things not apparently similar. Early poets, for instance, their thought richly imaginative, compared objects to people. They thus anthropomorphized nature by attributing to inanimate objects human qualities, such as emotion. The tendency to compare dissimilar things was, according to Vico, native to the human mind and a necessary imaginative precursor to more systematic or rational thought.

Vico called the metaphorical tendency of early human poets the "poetic mode of thought." He related the capacity for discovering metaphorical connections directly to "rhetorical 'wordplay', or 'wit' [*acutezza*]," also defined as acuteness or mental sharpness. The notion of *acutezza* was central to sixteenth and seventeenth century humanistic writing, and was best displayed in clever metaphors. Such rhetorical devices "can only come from an alert, imaginative mind, one with a well-honed facility for seeing connections between separate and apparently unrelated things." Thus, facility with words of the type taught in the rhetorical tradition was an aid to creative thought.

But Vico also urged that study of the traditional *topoi* of the classical rhetoricians contributes to quick and decisive thinking. Thus, he "sought to revive the 'art of topics,'" that is, he advocated study of the topical systems of classical rhetoric. He was particularly interested in the *stasis* systems of Quintilian and Cicero, built on a juridical model, that considered issues such as fact and definition. Vico's *Institutes of Oratory* (1711), the title itself drawn from that of Quintilian's *magnum opus,* treats these matters in detail. In short, Vico saw no better preparation for an active mind, one exhibiting the brilliance of *acutezza,* than the study of rhetoric.

From metaphor, "the primary operation of our mind," human thought progressed to metonym, the substitution of a part for the whole, an agent for an act, or of a sign for the thing signified. From *metonym,* thought, language, and literature moved to synecdoche, in which the whole object represents the part. Vico's final stage of linguistic development is irony, in which indirect statement carries direct meaning, or something is taken to stand for its opposite.

Thus, for Vico, the "sense-making" capacity that allowed human beings to create civilization out of disordered nature was exhibited in the imaginative fantasies of poets and storytellers rather than in the premises of philosophers or the deductions of logicians. In this way he reveals the influence of earlier Humanists. Vico writes that "fantasy collects from the senses and connects and enlarges to exaggeration the sensory effects of natural appearances and makes luminous images from them." That is, the imagination—guided naturally by rhetorical tropes—expands on the data of sense impressions and makes a distinctly *human* life possible. As the great French historian Paul Hazzard wrote, "If only Italy had listened to Giambattista Vico...our eighteenth century ancestors...would not have believed that reason was our first faculty, but on the contrary that imagination was."

BRITISH RHETORICS IN THE EIGHTEENTH CENTURY

We will begin our study of rhetoric in eighteenth-century Britain in the same place we have begun our discussion of rhetoric in other historical periods, with educational practice. Wilbur Samuel Howell writes that rhetoric was viewed in the eighteenth century as the means of transmitting knowledge from the learned to the general populace. Once established as the "master of the arts of popular discourse," rhetoric eventually staked a claim to being "the sole art of communication by means of language...." As such, rhetoric became particularly important to influential British educational movements in the eighteenth century. But, as we shall see, rhetorical concerns also were at the heart of philosophical and psychological thinking in this period. It is perhaps appropriate to note that though the theories that follow are often labeled "British" rhetorical theories, most of the thinkers described are Scottish, and one Irish. Thus, British should not be taken to mean English when applied to eighteenth-century rhetorical theory.

Rhetoric in British Education

British education in rhetoric was pursued during the eighteenth century with various goals in view, and in response to pressing social changes. Replying to rising skepticism in Britain, writers within the Churches of England and Scotland pressed rhetoric into the service of Christian apologetic, preaching, and writing. In addition, writing and reading of English prose began to assume a new prominence during the century as British culture shifted increasingly from oral to written discourse. Thus, the narrow conception of rhetoric as the study of speechmaking and argumentation was challenged, though the older view had its advocates as well.

Other changes taking place in eighteenth-century England assisted rhetoric's rise to prominence in education. English was displacing Latin as the language of scholarship, which allowed access to learning to a vastly increased number of British subjects. When Adam Smith began to lecture on rhetoric in 1748, "it was largely in response to a growing need for a comprehensive, thoroughly modern treatment of English and its uses...." Moreover, women were being admitted to the British universities in larger numbers during this period. Finally, urbanization was bringing people from the English countryside, from Scotland, and from Ireland to urban centers such as London. Many of these new city dwellers recognized that their rustic accents limited the possibility for personal advancement in the bigger cities. The corrective they sought was education in "proper" diction, which was an element of rhetorical education. Thus, education in rhetoric was sought out by an increasingly broad cross-section of the British public during the century.

The Emerging Public, and a Changing View of Rhetoric

The idea of "the public" needs to be emphasized, for during the eighteenth century a modern sense of both the public and the public domain were taking shape in Britain and Europe. Ordinary people could speak and write their opinions in a variety of new venues, and they could engage one another's ideas in a variety of settings. Whether in the public square, the meeting hall, the coffeehouse, or the newly popular periodicals of the day, citizen addressed citizen on a range of religious and political issues.

As a result of the expanding public domain and increasingly rhetorical public, a new understanding of rhetoric and oratorical skill gradually took hold as well. One ancient model that focused on winning a debate by any means available was losing ground. A new model that saw rhetoric as an important skill of public life was developing. Kenneth Cmiel writes that the Scottish rhetorical theorists of this period—George Campbell, Adam Smith, and others—"eschewed the manipulative goals of the Ciceronians. They argued that rhetoric should teach how to forcefully communicate one's reasoned arguments."

For a variety of reasons, then, rhetoric occupied a central place in British education in the eighteenth century. Winifred Horner notes that the potential for upward mobility in English society, a mobility dependent on a command of "good English," meant that there was a strong demand for language instruction, particularly instruction in writing. The rise of British nationalism in this period also encouraged instruction in English. Moreover, many Scottish and English educators were members of the clergy, and "education was understandably closely connected with religion." The strong emphasis on education in rhetoric spawned a variety of educational movements during the eighteenth and early nineteenth centuries.

THE ELOCUTIONARY MOVEMENT

Rhetoric has always been viewed, as we have noted at several points, as a means of personal advancement through the trained capacity to express one's views effectively, particularly in public settings. Throughout Western history, rhetoric has also functioned as a path to personal refinement and an avenue into polite social circles. The elocutionary movement of the eighteenth and nineteenth centuries draws our attention specifically to the performance side of rhetoric, and to rhetoric's use as a method for refining the public manners, poise, and expressiveness of men and women.

Eighteenth-century British society was relatively open for an individual's social advancement if we compare it with other European societies of the time. Coffeehouses, lodges, freethinking clubs, and debating societies attracted individuals from a striking mix of social classes. Women often participated in these public settings as well. Though class distinctions were still rather rigid, social movement was possible, particularly if one applied oneself to personal improvement. No improvement was more important than that of one's speech. Speech marked one as belonging to a particular social class. The goal of the aspiring young urbanite, then, was to speak like a gentleman or a lady.

Moreover, an increasing number of professions—law, politics, and religion in particular—demanded skill as a public speaker. Again, demand for instruction in this highly practical art grew. We might add that famous English essayists of the day, such as Richard Steele, Joseph Addison, and Jonathan Swift, had written critically of the quality of both speaking and writing in England. Such criticism lent some urgency to the search for instruction in proper and effective management of language. English education was simply not preparing students to explore and refine the great potential in the English tongue for eloquent expression.

Thomas Sheridan

As is so often the case, rhetoric answered a strongly felt social need in the second half of the eighteenth century. Thomas Sheridan (1719–1788), an Irish actor and educator, sought to provide the ready student with a guide to proper and effective public speaking. In fact, he sought nothing less than a general reform of education in Britain so as to correct what he took to be a very serious development—the neglect of elocution or rhetorical delivery. In *British Education* (1756), Sheridan wrote that poor preaching was actually threatening the health of religion.

So deep was Sheridan's belief in the beneficial effects of powerful public speaking that he maintained the study of elocution would, in the words of G. P. Mohrmann, "improve religion, morality, and constitutional government; would undergird a refining of the language, and would pave the way for ultimate perfection in all the arts." Sheridan wrote in *British Education* that oratory in the pulpit "must either effectually support religion against all opposition, or be the principal means of it's [sic] destruction."

The Importance of Delivery. Good delivery was intimately connected with convincing an audience of the urgency and truthfulness of one's message. "Before you can persuade a man into any opinion, he must first be convinced that you believe it yourself. This he can never be, unless the tones of voice in which you speak come from the heart, accompanied by corresponding looks, and gestures, which naturally result from a man who speaks in earnest."

Sheridan's deep concern about the poor quality of preaching in England is reflected in the following passage from his *A Discourse Introductory to a Course of Lectures* (1759):

> [A] man shall rise up in a public assembly, and, without the least mark of shame, deliver a discourse to many hundred auditors, in such disagreeable tones and unharmonious

cadences, as to disgust every ear; and with such improper and false use of emphasis, as to conceal or pervert the sense; and all without fear of any consequential disgrace.... [And] this is done...in the very service of the Most High!

Sheridan's most famous work, *A Course of Lectures on Elocution,* was published in 1762. This work was a compilation of lectures Sheridan had delivered at various sites around Great Britain. In *A Course of Lectures* he set out the principles of elocution as a rhetorical study and practice. Sheridan and other elocutionists emphasized delivery over the other traditional elements in the rhetorical art, such as invention or arrangement. Certainly training of the speaking voice was important to effective public presentations, as was the proper pronunciation of words. In fact, assisting young men from Ireland and Scotland to speak like educated English people so as to aid their success was one goal of the elocutionary movement. But, as one might expect from an actor, Sheridan did not view delivery simply as a matter involving the voice. Rather, the face and the body came into play in his discussion of the art of speaking in public. In fact, the instructions offered by elocutionists regarding facial expression, gesture, posture, and movement strike modern readers as something closer to instruction in acting, or even in dance, than in speaking.

Elocutionism's emphasis on delivery, and its use of teaching techniques such as the dramatic presentation of a memorized speech, led to a decline in concern for the argumentative or inventional function of rhetoric. Thus, a price was paid in the reduction of rhetoric's esteem for the benefit that came to some individuals through the honing of their presentational skills. Wilbur Samuel Howell writes that "the practices which the elocutionists encouraged inevitably led to declamation without sincere conviction and earnest feeling, as students recited discourses devised and organized by somebody else." Howell's summary statement is that elocutionism was a "strange movement" that turned out to be "futureless." Perhaps this reminds us that rhetoric is not simply a matter of appealing style and forceful delivery. Rhetoric divorced from the study of arguments and evidence becomes the practice of linguistic ornament.

THE SCOTTISH SCHOOL

In his excellent study, *Democratic Eloquence: The Fight over Popular Speech in Nineteenth-Century America,* Kenneth Cmiel notes the significant influence of a group of Scottish rhetorical theorists in the eighteenth century. Members of this Scottish school of rhetoric include George Campbell, Hugh Blair, Adam Smith, and others. Their new rhetorics affected British conceptions of eloquence and argument, but also shaped the teaching of rhetoric in America. Cmiel writes with regard to the early United States that "the texts of the Scottish school swept into the nation's classrooms to replace (or at least balance) the Ciceronian rhetoric used earlier. In 1783 Brown University ordered Blair's *Rhetoric* from England; in 1784 the first American edition was published." The following sections explore the new and rather different approaches to rhetoric of three Scottish theorists that were having such an impact on rhetorical education and practice.

The Belletristic Movement: Kames and Blair

During the eighteenth century, British interest in literature and writing expanded. Novels achieved a high degree of popularity, satisfying an increasing public desire to read for entertainment. Books were published that promised to help the would-be writer achieve clarity, grace, and beauty. Harold Harding has observed that "in the latter half of the eighteenth century more than fifty textbooks, essays, lectures, and treatises on rhetoric and literary criticism by thirty different writers were published in England, Ireland, and Scotland. Interest in literature and the teaching of writing ran high." Barbara Warnick has traced the French roots of the Belletristic Movement in Britain, suggesting that this emphasis on rhetorical style is not native to the British Isles. The study of belles lettres may, then, represent an eighteenth-century effect of Pierre Ramus' much earlier efforts to remove argument and invention from rhetoric.

The study of rhetoric both shaped and was shaped by this rapidly growing interest in literature, its structure, and its effects. A literary movement devoted to the advancement of what was termed *belles lettres* (beautiful letters or language) expanded rhetoric into a study of literature, literary criticism, and writing generally. Warnick writes "Belletristic rhetoric and studies of belles lettres were particularly concerned with examining the specific qualities of discourse and their effects." This approach to rhetoric "focused on reception, not production." This shift from rhetoric as the study of invention or "production" of arguments, to rhetoric as the study of *effects* on readers and listeners marks an important change of emphasis for rhetorical scholarship and education. The belletristic movement represents a change in rhetoric away from the classical emphasis on developing persuasive arguments for oral public discourse, and toward the educated reception or appreciation of written and spoken discourse.

Interest in *belles lettres* grew in the 1760s and 1770s, and was marked by an increased attention to matters of style as over against invention. Douglas Ehninger notes that "the rhetoric of belles lettres was given its classic and most influential expression in Hugh Blair's *Lectures on Rhetoric and Belles Lettres*" (1783). Other important writers and works in the movement include "William Barron's *Lectures on Belles Lettres and Logic* (London, 1806), and Alexander Jameison's *A Grammar of Rhetoric and Polite Literature* (London, 1818)." Ehninger adds that "in Lord Kame's *Elements of Criticism* (Edinburgh, 1762), some 500 pages of a combined 'rhetoric and poetic' were embedded in an inquiry into the nature of beauty and the foundations of taste." We will take a closer look at the work of two of these writers, Lord Kames and Hugh Blair.

Lord Kames. As rhetoric became more closely aligned with aesthetics, questions of taste and decorum became central to rhetorical theorizing. Some rhetorical theorists such as Henry Home (1696–1782), better known by his title, Lord Kames, returned to ancient principles like sublimity in their search for an aesthetic theory suited to a new era in British literature. Kames was a Scottish philosopher and lawyer whose interests also turned to matters of literary style and aesthetics. Following the Roman writer Longinus, Kames urged in his *The Elements of Criticism*

(1762) that the quality of sublimity was conveyed by "grand" or enormous objects such as a large tree, a high cliff, or an ocean. The emotion or state of mind experienced when in the presence of such an object could be approximated in writing that attended to such aesthetic concerns. Thus, Kames notes that Shakespeare achieved this effect in his play, *Julius Caesar:*

> The pleasant emotion raised by large objects, has not escaped the poets:
>
> *—He doth bestride the narrow world*
> *Like a Colossus; and we petty men*
> *Walk under his huge legs.*
>
> *Julius Caesar, Act I, Sc. 3.*

Kames also devotes a great deal of attention in the second chapter of *The Elements of Criticism* to the matter of arousing emotions, particularly through an appeal to the reader's sense of beauty. Kames pursued the notion of verbal beauty to the point of exploring the effects that the various spoken sounds have on hearers. For example, he writes with great specificity about the effects of sounds in particular words and word combinations:

> In the first place, syllables in immediate succession, pronounced each of them with the same or nearly the same aperture of the mouth, produce a succession of weak and feeble sounds; witness the French words *dit-il, pathetique:* on the other hand, a syllable of the greatest aperture succeeding one of the smallest, on the contrary, makes a succession which, because of its remarkable disagreeableness, is distinguished by a proper name, *hiatus.* The most agreeable succession is, where the cavity is increased and diminished alternately within moderate limits. Examples, *alternative, longevity, pusillanimous.*

Like others in the Belletristic Movement, Kames was intrigued with the notion of "taste." Taste, or the ability to recognize and appreciate high quality in literature and other art, was in Kames's view a largely natural quality of some individuals. One would not search for taste among "those who depend for food on bodily labor," for example. If this sounds like an elitist idea, it is. Kames envisioned a refined society of individuals capable of appreciating the finer artistic achievements in literature and art. Such individuals were born, not made, though inborn capacities could be refined through proper education. As Warnick writes, "in Kames' theory is manifest an elitism that lies just below the surface of Scottish views on taste but is rarely openly articulated."

Kames' interests point up again that rhetoric and a concern for written and spoken style are difficult to separate. Aristotle devoted his last book in *Rhetoric* to a consideration of stylistic matters. Moreover, at times in the history of rhetoric, matters of style become rhetoric's principal focus. Recall the Sophist Gorgias' efforts to discover a style of writing and speaking that would allow him to manipulate his audiences, to become a *psychagogos.* Kames' desire to understand the mechanisms by which speech affects thought and emotion is not far removed as a matter of inquiry, though it may be far removed in motive.

Hugh Blair. Hugh Blair (1718–1800) was a Scottish preacher, born and educated in Edinburgh, who made important contributions to the Belletristic Movement. A famous Presbyterian preacher, in 1762 Blair was appointed to the Regius Chair of Rhetoric and Belles Lettres at the University of Edinburgh. In 1783 he published his most famous work, the *Lectures on Rhetoric and Belles Lettres.* This work was widely read in England and abroad, and went through numerous editions. Blair was a student of English literature, and an editor of Shakespeare's works. Style, taste, beauty, and decorum are central to Blair's rhetorical theory, as they were to that of Kames. And, like Kames, Blair returns to several ancient rhetoricians for ideas—writers like Aristotle, Cicero, Longinus, and Quintilian.

It is probably not an exaggeration to say that Blair wrote his *Lectures* with the goal in mind of improving the lives of his students. Much as Cicero's "perfect orator" was a person of eloquence, wisdom, grace, charm, and wit, so Blair's students developed the qualities of taste, eloquence, critical acumen, and style. Rhetoric's educational goals, then, are broader than simple preparation for professional success through making effective speeches. Rhetorical training is preparation for living the good life, the life that combines graceful and effective expression in the public sphere with contemplation and enhanced aesthetic experience in the private. However, Cicero's *perfectus orator* is a dynamic public figure employing extraordinary rhetorical skill for the greater good of society. Blair's is a more parochial, even private model—the individual citizen pursuing personal grace, leisure enjoyment, and social advancement. Much of Blair's work strikes a contemporary reader as arcane, but there is an unmistakable sincerity of conviction about the goals of education that probably should not be quickly dismissed.

As rhetorical interests grew from strictly spoken discourse to include written, a corresponding shift occurred in the perceived domain of rhetoric. Rhetoric was no longer seen as an art pertinent only to public affairs. Rhetoric was becoming part of private life as well.

Taste and Style. This shift from public to private worlds is evident in Blair's references to the notion of taste, a developed appreciation of aesthetic experiences. Though taste is in part a matter of "natural sensibility to beauty," Blair is convinced that this capacity can be improved through experience and education. Thus, Blair urges on his readers the development of their capacity for taste toward the enhancement of their private lives, their lives beyond work. "The cultivation of taste is farther recommended, by the happy effects which it naturally tends to produce in human life," writes Blair, especially in one's private life. People who live "in the most active sphere" of public life, "cannot be always occupied by business," he argues. Moreover, persons "of serious professions cannot always be on the stretch of serious thought," that is, cannot always devote their mental energies to serious topics and demanding problems. Thus, the development of taste, which enhances the enjoyment of diversions such as literature, is recommended to Blair's students as a means balancing the demands of work and the public sphere, with the retreat and enjoyments of private life.

Blair defines style as "the peculiar manner in which a man expresses his conceptions, by means of language." Thus, style is for Blair a very broad category of concern. Moreover, style is related to one's "manner of thinking." Thus, "when we are examining an author's composition, it is, in many cases, extremely difficulty to separate the Style from the sentiment." Blair was apparently of the opinion, then, that one's style—one's manner of linguistic expression—provided evidence of how one thought.

There are only two considerations to which the critic or student of style should attend. Blair calls these "perspicuity and ornament." "For," he writes, "all that can possibly be required of Language, is, to convey our ideas clearly to the minds of others, and, at the same time, in such a dress, as by pleasing and interesting them, shall most effectually strengthen the impressions which we seek to make." Practical matters, then, are at the heart of the study of style for Blair. Rhetoric seeks to make a point persuasively. Thus, rhetorical style must attract an audience and present a case clearly. This is not bad advice to any writer or speaker, and Blair spends a good deal of time trying to explain how to make language both attractive and clear.

Of perspicuity, or clarity, Blair writes that there is no concern more central to style. After all, if clarity is lacking in a message, all is lost. Claiming that your subject is difficult is no excuse for lack of clarity according to Blair: if you can't explain a difficult subject clearly, you probably don't understand it. Blair's advice on clarity includes selecting precisely the right terms to make your point, avoiding "obsolete or new-coined words," and always speaking in a manner appropriate to your audience and your subject. Much of Blair's counsel to his young readers includes such reminders as "any words, which do not add some importance to the meaning of a Sentence, always spoil it." This is still good advice.

George Campbell

Some British Enlightenment rhetoricians developed new approaches to rhetoric out of a curiosity about what rhetoric revealed about the human mind. The world of the mind was beginning to be mapped using new philosophical approaches, and rhetoric was seen by some as a means of expanding our understanding of human thought itself. John Locke's psychological speculations were highly influential in scholarly circles early in the eighteenth century, while David Hume's discussion of the nature of human thought, in his *Enquiries* (1748), dominated philosophical and psychological scholarship during the second half of the century.

George Campbell (1719–1796) was one of the most important rhetorical theorists of the late eighteenth century. Like several other influential English-speaking philosophers and rhetorical theorists of his day, Campbell was Scottish. Scotland's university cities—Edinburgh, Glasgow, and Aberdeen—were sites of great intellectual activity in the eighteenth century. Campbell was born in Aberdeen, where he received his early education. Later, he attended Marischal College in Aberdeen, where he studied law. His interests, however, turned toward theology, and he pursued a course of studies to prepare himself to be a minister. In 1748 he was ordained to the clergy of the Church of Scotland. In 1758 he was appointed principal of Marischal

College, and later, in 1771, he was elevated to the important position of professor of Divinity at the same school. Campbell was a practicing religious polemicist who entered late into the great Deist controversy. His famous *Dissertation on Miracles* (1762) was a response to David Hume's argument against miracles. Campbell's most important work in rhetoric was his *The Philosophy of Rhetoric,* published in 1776. Another important work related to rhetoric was his *Lectures on Pulpit Eloquence.*

A Scientific Rhetoric. As we have already noted, much of Campbell's work on rhetoric incorporates British philosophical thought of the seventeenth and eighteenth centuries. Campbell's writing reveals the influence both of those philosophers with whom he agreed on various matters, and those with whom he took issue, especially Hobbes. Though he disagreed sharply with David Hume on a number of issues, Campbell admitted a great debt to the philosopher. In fact, the leading authority of Campbell's work, Lloyd Bitzer, writes that "Campbell's philosophy and his theory of human nature, both of which profoundly affect his treatment of rhetoric, are drawn mainly from Hume." Campbell intended to offer a new rhetoric, one incorporating insights of the Enlightenment period. At the same time, he believed that he was building on the classical tradition in rhetoric by providing scientific support for classical insights. But he also hoped to move beyond those insights.

Rhetoric and philosophy were inseparably linked for Campbell, as the title of his work, *The Philosophy of Rhetoric,* suggests. Moreover, Campbell often tested his ideas on rhetoric by reading papers before the Aberdeen Philosophical Society, which he had helped to found. This Society also included thinkers such as Thomas Reid, James Beattie, and Alexander Gerard. Bitzer notes, however, that Hume "was the leading figure in the intellectual movement in which Campbell conceived and tested nearly the whole of his *The Philosophy of Rhetoric.*

Campbell advanced a "scientific" rhetoric, but *science* for him meant something like what philosophy means today: an organized and rational account of a subject. "All art is founded on science," he writes in the introduction to *The Philosophy of Rhetoric,* but he counts as "the most sublime of all sciences" the studies of "*theology* and *ethics.*" His rhetoric, then, reflects what were taken to be advances in fields such as ethics and psychology. "It was widely believed in the eighteenth century, even by defenders of the Ancients," writes George Kennedy, "that modern philosophy had made tremendous strides beyond the past." Campbell thus sought, through new discoveries, to understand how the human mind operates and to provide instruction in eloquence based on that understanding. His interest in applying new knowledge to the study of rhetoric also meant that the classical sources—Aristotle, Cicero, and Quintilian—became less important to rhetorical theory than they had been in the Middle Ages and Renaissance.

Rhetoric and Psychology. Campbell connected eloquence to psychology. He defines eloquence as "that art or talent by which the discourse is adapted to its end." Campbell's "theory of eloquence" was based on the belief that the mind is moved "only by those ideas it accepts as truthful and good." Thus, as noted above, he sought a science of eloquence founded on the science of psychology. Campbell's rhetorical theory reflects the psychology current in Britain in the eighteenth century. Influenced by Locke, theorists divided up the mind into different capacities or "faculties." In the faculty psychology view, the mind consisted of the understanding, the imagination, the passions, and the will.

For Campbell, each mental faculty spoke virtually its own language. For instance, the understanding spoke the language of logic, while the passion spoke the language of emotion. Each part also performed a distinct function. The understanding was informed and, when satisfied, responded with conviction. The imagination perceived beauty. The passions and will moved one toward action. Thus, each faculty has a part to play in the persuasive process. As he writes, "all the ends of speaking are reducible to four; every speech being intended to enlighten the understanding, to please the imagination, to move the passions, or to influence the will." The relationship between eloquence and mental faculties was central to Campbell's thinking about rhetoric. "In both *The Philosophy of Rhetoric* and *Lectures on Pulpit Eloquence*," writes Barbara Warnick, "Campbell's principal aim was to describe how style and expression contributed to discourse's ability to appeal to the various faculties of its hearers."

Two Types of Reasoning: Scientific and Moral. Campbell discussed two types of reasoning that engage the faculty of the understanding: scientific and moral. Scientific reasoning, or the use of syllogistic logic, deals with demonstrable propositions of the type one encounters in mathematics and formal logic. It moves by demonstration from first principles or *axioms* to necessary conclusions or conclusions about which there can be no doubt.

But Campbell found syllogistic logic inappropriate to the kind of questions with which rhetoric typically deals. He was particularly concerned, then, with moral reasoning, by which he meant reasoning from evidence to more or less probable conclusions on practical issues. We rely on moral reasoning in making practical decisions, and in most of the arenas of thought that make up daily life: politics, religion, economics. Certainty of the type sought in scientific reasoning is simply not possible given the nature of the questions and evidence with which moral reasoning typically deals, matters of faith and conduct, for instance. We reason from the available evidence to the best conclusions possible.

Campbell offers a treatment of evidence in Book I, Chapter V of *The Philosophy of Rhetoric*. His discussion takes in everything from consciousness and common sense to experience, analogy, testimony, and even statistics or "the calculation of chances." In moral reasoning, there is often more than one side or case that can advance evidence in its support. A clash of views results, in a manner typical of rhetorical discourse.

A Theory of Persuasion. One of Campbell's more famous contributions to the history of rhetoric is his theory of persuasion. As Howell explains, "[T]wo things must be done, he said, by an author who would persuade others." The first, according to Campbell, "is to excite some desire or passion in the hearers; the second is, to satisfy their judgment, that there is a connection between the action to which he would persuade them, and the gratification of the desire of passion which he excites."

Campbell held persuasion to be a matter of addressing both the emotions and the reason, as people are not convinced without arguments and do not act except in response to emotions. "When persuasion is the end, passion [emotion] must be engaged," he writes. Campbell explains the relationships between emotion and reason this way: "The former is effected by communicating lively and glowing ideas of the object; the latter...by presenting the best and most forcible arguments which the nature of the subject admits." Thus, a speaker must know how to craft lively or "vivacious" images addressed to the passions and forceful arguments for the understanding.

Important to Campbell's thinking about persuasion was the notion of plausibility. A plausible discourse was instantly believable because of its close association with an audience's experience of their social world. As Warnick writes, "Plausibility went beyond the chronological sequencing of events in Campbell's theory.... He viewed it as arising from any description in which what was portrayed conformed to experience and expectation so as to appeal to the audience's imagination." Plausibility was the feature in an orator's narration of events that corresponded to "probability" in the presentation of "sound arguments and the use of facts." Thus, persuasion was a product of the probability of one's arguments, and the plausibility of one's narratives.

Education in Eloquence. Howell writes that "rhetoric and eloquence are synonymous terms with [Campbell]." Thus, he was concerned that his students learn from the art of rhetoric both elocution—the ability to speak with grace, force, and clarity—and argumentation. They must know how to present a message clearly and attractively, as well how to defend a proposition with sound inference and solid evidence. Campbell's "Christian orator" had a more demanding task than did the political and judicial orators of ancient times. Why is this? Because "it is not a momentary but a permanent effect at which he aims...a thorough change of heart and disposition." No demand on eloquence could be greater than "to persuade [a multitude] for the love of God, to be wise, and just and good."

Of particular importance to achieving eloquence was the kind of descriptive language that would engage the imagination. Much of what we believe comes not through direct experience, but through a clear and convincing appeal to the imagination. Thus, rhetoric's appeal to imagination is crucial to persuasion. As Warnick writes, "Campbell...reminds his readers that oratory is, in a sense, painting, and that an orator must exhibit lively and glowing images of his subjects so as to bring his auditor's imaginations to the point where their representations will impress the mind as do the stimulations of sense and memory." This capacity to affect the imagination is one sign of true eloquence.

Campbell's rhetoric had practical goals, and was tied most directly to the practical concerns of a public figure—the Christian minister. But any effective speaker, in Campbell's analysis, must understand both the human mind and the resources of language that can engage the mind so as to move the listener to action.

Section Ten: Ethics and Rhetoric

SECTION TEN: ETHICS AND RHETORIC

Ethics

Robert Solomon

"From now on I'm thinking only of me."
Major Danby replied indulgently with a superior smile,
"But Yossarian, suppose everyone felt that way?"
"Then I'd certainly be a —— fool to feel any
other way, wouldn't I?"

Joseph Heller, *Catch 22*

What should we do? And what should we not do? What acts should we praise? What acts should we condemn and blame? These are questions of **ethics,** the concern for which made Socrates willing to give up his life. The core of ethics is **morality.** Morality is a set of fundamental rules that guide our actions; for example, they may forbid us to kill each other, encourage us to help each other, tell us not to lie, command us to keep our promises.

Most of the moral rules we accept and follow are ones that we have learned and uncritically adopted from parents, friends, teachers, and our own society. At times, though, others may challenge our moral rules, demanding that we defend them. Why should we help each other? Why shouldn't we ever cheat? What reasons can we give to defend one sexual ethic rather than another? New social and technological developments may also force us to reevaluate our morality. Pressure from minorities and women for equal rights has forced many to reconsider the justice of discrimination on the basis of race or sex. And the development of sophisticated life-sustaining devices has forced both physicians and philosophers to question whether it is always a moral duty to preserve life (and refrain from killing).

Whenever we try to defend or criticize a moral belief we enter the realm of ethics. Ethics is not concerned with specific moral rules but with the foundation of morality and with providing very general principles that will both help us evaluate the validity of a moral rule and choose between different moralities (different sets of moral rules). For example, some ethical theorists called **utilitarians** hold that any good moral rule should promote the greatest happiness for the greatest number. Other theorists, for example, Aristotle and Kant, have argued that a good moral rule helps us act in the most rational way possible.

Ethics is also concerned with deciding whether we should take into account others' or our own interests and desires when deciding what we ought to do. For some ethicists, morality is tied to self-interest at least in an abstract way, and they argue that morality is the best way of satisfying everyone's interests. Other philosophers retain the rigid distinction between morality and self-interest and insist that obedience to morality is good for its own sake, or equivalent to being rational, or simply required in order to make us human. Finally some authors have argued that morality is only one among many sets of principles, which we may but need not choose to obey.

In this chapter, we will begin by raising some of the perennial problems of ethics, including the nature of morality and the problem of moral relativism. Then, we will address the familiar claim that the basis of all human behavior—moral behavior included—is selfishness, or **egoism.** Finally we will examine several different ethical theories, different ways of conceiving of morals and (or) justifying moral beliefs:

—The ethics of Aristotle, who based his view of morality on the concept of "virtue" and his idea that man is by nature a social and rational animal. Aristotle argues that being virtuous—controlling our feelings and acting rationally—enables us to become fully human. In this discussion, we have the opportunity to examine a moral system that is significantly different from our own, but still sufficiently similar for us to understand it.

—The view that morality is essentially a matter of feeling; David Hume and Jean-Jacques Rousseau are its representatives.

—The monumental ethical theory of Immanuel Kant, who insisted that morality is strictly a matter of practical reason, divorced from our personal interests and desires and based solely on universal principles or laws. Thus, according to Kant, we cannot justify the morality of our actions by appealing to the good consequences our actions have for others or ourselves.

—The ethical theories of the utilitarians, who argued (in contrast to Kant) that moral rules were merely rules of thumb for achieving the greatest good for the greatest number of people, and who thereby tried to reconcile the interests of each individual with the interests of everyone else.

—The radical theories of Nietzsche and the existentialists, who insist that, in an important sense, we choose our moralities and that this choice cannot be justified in any of the ways argued by other modern philosophers. For Nietzsche, at least, this view also included a retrospective appreciation of the morality of the ancient Greeks, and he argued that we should inject some of their conceptions into our own.

—The "metaethical" theories of G. E. Moore and A. J. Ayer, and the implications of these for practical ethics.

MORALITY

Morality gives us the rules by which we live with other people. It sets limits to our desires and our actions. It tells us what is permitted and what is not. It gives us guiding principles for making decisions. It tells us what we ought and what we ought not to do. But what is this "morality" that sounds so impersonal and "above" us? It is important to begin with an appreciation for the metaphor, which so well characterizes moral rules. Nietzsche describes it this way: "A tablet of virtues hangs over every people."

This "tablet of virtues" is morality. The prototype of morality, in this view, is those ancient codes, carved in stone, with commands that are eternal and absolute. We know best the two tablets inscribed by God, in front of Moses, which we call the Ten Commandments. And they are indeed *commandments.* "Thou shalt" and "Thou shalt not" is all they say. And this is the essence of morality. It consists of commands. These commands do not appeal to individual pleasures or desires. They do not make different demands on different individuals or societies. Quite to the contrary, they are absolute rules that tell us what we must or must not do, no matter who we are, no matter what we want, and regardless of whether or not our interests will be served by the command. "Thou shalt not kill" means that even if you want to, even if you have the power to, and even if you can escape all punishment, you are absolutely forbidden to kill.

The image of morality as coming "from above" is appropriate. First, because moral laws are often said, and not only in our society, to come from God. Second, because we learn these laws from our parents, who literally "stand over us" and indoctrinate us with them through their shouts, commands, examples, threats, and gestures. Finally and most importantly, morality itself is "above" any given individual or individuals, whether it is canonized in the laws of society or not. Morality is not just another aid in getting us what we want; it is entirely concerned with right and wrong. And these considerations are "above" tampering by any individual, no matter how powerful, as if they have a life of their own.

This characteristic of morality as independent of individual desires and ambitions has led many people to characterize morality simply in terms of some absolute and independent agency. Most often, this absolute and independent agency is God. Saint Augustine, for example, talks about morality in this way.

> ... Unless you turn to Him and repay the existence that He gave you, you won't be "nothing"; you will be wretched. All things owe to God, first of all, what they are insofar as they are natures. Then, those who have received a will owe to Him whatever better thing they can will to be, and whatever they ought to be. No man is ever blamed for what he has not been given, but he is justly blamed if he has not done what he should have done; and if he has received free will and sufficient power, he stands under obligation. When a man does not do what he ought, God the Creator is not at fault. It is to His glory that a man suffers justly; and by blaming a man for not doing what he should have done, you are praising what he ought to do. You are praised for seeing what you ought to do, even though you see this only through God, who is immutable Truth.[1]

And St. Thomas Aquinas: " ... It is apparent that things prescribed by divine law are right, not only because they are put forth by law, but also because they are in accord with nature." Or "Therefore by divine law precepts had to be given, so that each man would give his neighbor his due and would abstain from doing injuries to him."[2] And in the Bible: "When thou shalt harken—to the voice of the Lord thy God, to keep all his commandments, which I command thee this day, to do that which is right in the Eyes of the Lord thy God."[3]

But whether or not one believes in God, it is clear that something further is needed to help us define morality. Even assuming that there is a God, we need a way of determining what His moral commands must be. One might say that He has given these commands to various individuals, but the fact is that different people seem to have very different ideas about the morality that God has given them. Some, for example, would say that it explicitly rules out abortion and infanticide. Others would argue that God does not rule these out but makes it clear that they are, like other forms of killing (a "holy war," for example), justifiable only in certain circumstances. And in view of such disagreements, we cannot simply appeal to God but must, for reasons that we can formulate and defend, define our morality for ourselves. There is the further question, which has often been debated, whether we should follow God's laws just because they are His or rather, whether God is good because His laws are good. If the latter, then we have to decide what is good in order to know that God is good. If the former, then one has to decide whether or not to believe in God precisely on the basis of whether we can accept those laws. Either way, we have to decide for ourselves what laws of morality we are willing to accept.

Similar considerations hold true for that familiar appeal to conscience in determining what we ought or ought not do. Even if one believes that conscience is God-given, the same problems emerge again. Should we follow our consciences just because "conscience tells us to"? Or do we follow our conscience just because we know that what our conscience commands is good. How does one decide whether a nagging thought is or is not the prompting of God? Probably on the basis of whether what it demands is good or not. (Thus one readily attributes to conscience the nagging reminder that one shouldn't have cheated an unsuspecting child, but one does not attribute to conscience the nagging thought that one could have gotten away with shoplifting if only one had had the daring to do it.) If one believes that conscience is simply the internalization of the moral teachings of one's parents and society, then the question takes an extra dimension: Should we accept or reject what we have been taught? Since our consciences often disagree, we must still decide whose conscience and which rules of conscience one ought to obey. Identifying morality with the promptings of one's conscience is both plausible and valuable, but philosophically it only moves the question one step back: how do we know what is, and what is not, the prompting of conscience? And is it always right to follow one's conscience? But these two questions are in fact just another way of asking, what is moral? What should I do?

Morality is not just obedience—whether obedience to the king, the Pope, the law or one's conscience. Morality is doing what is *right*, whether or not it is commanded by any person or law and whether or not one "feels" it in one's conscience. One way of putting this—defended later on by Immanuel Kant—is to say that morality involves **autonomy**, that is, the ability to think for oneself and decide, for oneself, what is right and what is wrong, whom to obey and whom to ignore, what to do and what not to do. The danger is that this conception of morality as autonomy seems to leave us without a place to learn morality in the first place. How do we learn to judge right and wrong but from our parents, our friends, our teachers, and our society and its models? But if we try to tie morality too closely to our upbringing and our society, then it looks as if there is no room for autonomy, no way in which we could disagree with our family or society, no way to criticize the way in which we have been raised. Furthermore, tying morality to particular societies raises an additional question, and that is whether morality (or morali*ties*) might not be **relative** to particular societies and cultures.

IS MORALITY RELATIVE?

Moralities, like lifestyles, vary from culture to culture and even from person to person. But while there is nothing surprising about the fact that lifestyles vary, there is a problem in the variation of moralities. Morality, by its very nature, is supposed to be a set of universal principles, principles that do not distinguish between cultures or peoples or lifestyles. If it is morally reprehensible to kill for fun, then it is morally reprehensible in every society, in every culture, for every lifestyle, and for every person, no matter who he or she is. And this will be true even if the society or person in question does not agree with that moral principle. Aristotle, for example, discusses at length what he calls "the wicked man," who does evil because he believes in immoral principles and therefore acts without regret, unlike the person who acts badly from momentary weakness, force of circumstances, desperation, or misinformation. But on what grounds can one society or person claim that another society's or person's principles are immoral? How could European Christians, for example, be justified in criticizing the sexual morality of Polynesians in the South Pacific? The Polynesians were a separate society, with their own mores and principles that worked quite well for them, possibly even better in certain ways than the European customs worked in Europe. Yet European missionaries felt no hesitation whatever in condemning their sexual practices as "immoral." And similarly but more seriously, what gives us the right to criticize a culture across the world that still believes in genocide as a legitimate consequence of war or in torture as a way of keeping civil order? We surely feel that we have the right to speak up in such cases, but then we too are asserting the universality of our morality, extending it even to people who might explicitly reject our principles. How can we do this? What justifies such an extension?

The problem of relativism has become extremely controversial since the nineteenth century, when anthropologists began telling us of exotic societies with moralities so different from ours. In a sense, relativism has always been a threat to established morality, for even the Greeks came into contact with societies that were much different from theirs. (Thus their tendency to immediately label anything non-Greek "barbarian," so that they didn't have to consider the possibility of relativism.) Kant was the most vigorous opponent of relativism, for his conception of morality was such that if a human being was to count as rational at all, he or she had to agree to at least the basic principles of a universal morality. There were people and societies that did not, but that, according to Kant, only proved that they were less than rational (and therefore less than human as well). Today we tend to be more liberal in our acceptance of different styles of life, but few people would deny that at least some moral principles hold for every society. The principle that unnecessary cruelty is wrong, for example, would be such a principle, although people might well disagree about what was "cruel" and what was "unnecessary."

Philosophers generally distinguish two theses. First, there is the factual claim that different societies have different moralities. This is called **cultural relativism.** The difficult question is whether these different moralities are only different superficially or whether they are fundamentally different. For example, Eskimos of certain tribes kill their elders by leaving them to freeze on the ice; we consider that grossly immoral (we send most of our elders to frigid "old-age homes" instead). But the question of cultural relativity is whether this difference is merely the reflection of different interpretations of some basic moral principle (such as, don't kill anyone unless it is absolutely necessary for the survival of the rest) or whether it really is a wholly different morality. This is among the most controversial anthropological questions of our time. But philosophers are interested in a somewhat different question: Assuming that two moralities really are fundamentally different, is it possible that each is as correct as the other? The philosopher who says "yes" is an **ethical relativist.** And it is ethical relativism that will occupy us here.

In the following selection, the English-American philosopher Walter Stace presents the ethical relativist position and its traditional opponent, **ethical absolutism,** the view that there is only one correct morality. Stace's own answer to the problem is more of an absolutist solution; later in the same work he says that "happiness" is a universal and absolute value, and therefore cross-cultural evaluations are possible.

Notes

[1]St. Augustine, *On Freedom* (New York: Bobbs-Merrill, 1956).
[2]St. Thomas Aquinas, *Summa Contra Gentiles*, Bk. III (New York: Doubleday, 1955).
[3]Deuteronomy, 13:18.

Section Eleven: Existentialism and Rhetoric

Section Eleven: Existentialism and Rhetoric

The Existential Revolt against Modernists

Craig R. Smith

One of the major themes of this text is that rhetoric is a response to uncertainty. The modern philosophers, like the scholastics who preceded them, tried to end uncertainty by combining the discoveries of science and psychology with rationalism. Their aim was progress and a consensus among experts as to what the truth was. Their line of thinking could be traced back through the scholastics and Plato to the naturalists of ancient Greece. However, just as with previous truth-based theories, the modernists' philosophy was assailed by lingering doubts. Uncertainty sustained the need for rhetoric both as a discourse that could make the unclear lucid and as a form of communication that could make sense of the world.

Another theme of this text has been that for every major school of thought, another school of thought forms in reaction. The naturalists of ancient Greece developed theories in reaction to the mythologists who had preceded them. In attacking the Sophists, Plato became one of the most influential thinkers in the history of the world; Neoplatonism flourished for centuries. Humanists fought the exclusivity of the rigid logical approach of the scholastics. Thus, it should come as no surprise that there have been several revolts against the objectivism and rationalism of "modernist" philosophy. While Hume's "scepticism" certainly put cracks in the modernist facade, this doctrine was not adopted as a means for existing in the world. Questioning all knowledge is fine on a theoretical level, but at some point one must get on with one's life and make decisions based on the information at hand.

Perhaps no philosophy is more concerned with everyday existence and decision making than existentialism. Before we can understand its relevance to rhetoric, we need a clearer picture of the positions against which the existentialists were revolting. This chapter begins by exemplifying modernist thinking by reviewing the contributions of Immanuel Kant and Georg F. W. Hegel, who built on the philosophers we examined in the previous chapter. It then examines the thinking of the five most significant existential philosophers in an effort to deduce a rhetorical theory. In the process, we shall examine rhetoric's role in the quest for transcendent spirit and authenticity in everyday existence, two major goals of existential philosophers.

THE MODERNIST POSITION

Perhaps the best examples of modernist thinkers are Immanuel Kant (1724–1804) and Georg Wilhelm Friedrich Hegel (1770–1831). Kant received his Ph.D. in 1755 at the University of Königsberg in Prussia, where he lived off the fees students paid him for his lectures as they prepared for their examinations. He eventually became a professor of logic and metaphysics at the university. While his work on metaphysics was enormously influential, his more humanistic works were largely ignored. For example, his *Lectures on Ethics* was not published in English until 1924.

Like Kant, Hegel supported himself by tutoring until he was appointed to a professorship at the University of Jena in his native Germany. Forced to flee Napoleon's army, Hegel moved to Nuremberg where he taught high school and wrote his *Science of Logic* (1812–16), in which he claimed in the "Introduction" that logic was the reflection of God before the creation of nature. After a brief teaching stint in Heidelberg, the success of the book led to his appointment at the University of Berlin. His reputation brought students from all over Europe to study with him until his death in 1831.

These two major philosophers believed that you could determine the truth and achieve your highest aim through rational mental processes. Hegel believed freedom was the ultimate good and claimed that one could get to it by using reason alone. He applied Aristotle's dialectic approach to history to demonstrate that it is driven by the *clash of thesis and anti-thesis*. The result is a new *synthesis* which preserves the best elements of the thesis and anti-thesis. In fact, Hegel believed that every thesis implied an anti-thesis. The thesis, "We should go to war," implies the anti-thesis, "We should not go to war." Relevant evidence and arguments were mounted in favor of and against each thesis and anti-thesis. In the ensuing attack and response, the false would be revealed and the true would be retained. The surviving residue is a synthesis, which now becomes a new thesis: "Under certain circumstances, we should go to war." Many found this optimistic use of dialectic to be attractive, including Karl Marx (see chapter 10) who converted it into an engine of criticism known as "dialectical materialism."

Hegel's optimistic approach to history was inspired by Comte Henri de Saint-Simon, who believed that civilization had reached its highest, most mature stage. Hegel claimed that in each stage, a larger and larger percentage of the population enjoyed the fruits of freedom. More progress was possible, however, if we learned the lessons of history and allowed each nation to follow its own "spirit" to freedom. To accomplish this, Hegel adapted his dialectical method to history. A thesis, which could be represented as an entrenched group or established institution, was attacked by an anti-thesis, represented by a reform or revolutionary group. History revealed to Hegel that the result of the clash was never a total victory for either side. Instead, a synthesis emerged which was an improvement over the thesis and a better embodiment of the national "spirit" of freedom.

In this way, Hegel tried to show that history was dialectically dynamic; it was neither static nor did it repeat itself. It was a rational upward spiral toward freedom for greater and greater numbers of people. This evolutionary notion was a clear extension of enlightenment thinking which placed so much faith in the reasoning ability of humans to bring order to free societies. It also inspired a new wave of Romantic philosophers and artists who fought for self-determination of national groups. The poet Lord Byron, for example, fought for Greek independence. Hegel's position came to dominate most German universities immediately following his death.

Instead of national spirit, Kant sought to uncover the universal morality God had provided to humans. He attempted this by using reason alone. Thus, the modern era of rationalism tried to replace the religious era, which rang with Luther's paraphrase of Paul, "Justification by faith alone." Spiritual slavery and religious wars were to be replaced by human reason and individual critiques that were highly skeptical. In fact, perhaps because his father was Scottish, Kant was greatly influenced by Hume's "scepticism." Hence Kant's book is called *Religion within the Limits of Reason Alone*, a refutation of Luther's famous phrase.

Kant was a deeply religious and popular lecturer in Prussia who never published a major work until he was forty-six. Yet he strongly influenced thinkers who followed him by providing a *Critique of Pure Reason* (1781), which argued that ethical systems should be grounded in reason and only then traced to moral consciousness. Kant's call for an abstract kind of intellection undermined the blind dogma of some religious thinkers. Kant claimed the mind was powerful enough to order its sensed experiences and relate them to time and space; he called this the "Transcendental Aesthetic." The "Transcendental Logic" is what organizes the concepts we perceive. Both are universal characteristics in humans and dubbed "transcendental" because they rise above common ways of knowing things. The mind is also capable of filling in a fuller picture of what it perceives. For example, if you see someone from behind, you may recognize certain characteristics such as a particular swagger or hair style and reach a conclusion as to the identity of the person without seeing his or her face. You will fill in the face, even though it is unseen. Thus, "pure reason" is not possible; to be useful and correct, reason requires the real objects of the world to stimulate rational mental processes.

In this way, Kant revealed the influence of Locke on his thinking: we come to know reality by first-hand contact with it; intuition is an immediate relation of knowledge to objects. Appearances are created in the mind when it orders numerous sensations. Intuition gives us immediate and unique experiences; understanding gives us universal categories for the ordering of what we sense. Reality is phenomena, and reason is not possible without relating it to this reality, hence Kant's condemnation of "pure reason as an abstraction."

We rationally apprehend and interpret what our intuition produces in the mind. This interpretation is made possible by categories of reason that operate universally in humans. Kant's "categorical imperative" drove the modern move to make reason a primary grounding of all truth. This led to Kant's publication of a *Critique of Practical Reason* in 1788, which supports a moral view of the world that can be obtained by reason.

Kant was quick to point out that there is also an ineffable "noumenal" reality beyond the practical world. Like Plato's noumenal world, it contains different and higher truths; unlike Plato, however, Kant did not believe humans were capable of perceiving it. Nonetheless, it provides a metaphysical and religious escape hatch which prevented Kant from being too severely censored by his ruler, Frederick the Great of Prussia. For example, Kant argued that while human intuition will confirm that causality rules the phenomenal world, in the noumenal world it is possible that complete freedom exists.

When properly grounded in the real world, the use of reason produces a voice of duty that is a "categorical imperative." This duty is the human respect for law which animal instincts cannot provide. Said Kant, "Act only according to that maxim by which you can at the same time will that it should become a universal law." Thus, all moral decisions require the use of reason to determine their universal nature.

EXISTENTIAL OBJECTIONS

One of the most interesting things about existentialism is the number of times it is hyphenated with other terms in order to explain what is being advocated. There are Christian-existentialists and atheistic-existentialists; there are monological-existentialists and interrelational-existentialists. Some critics argue that Shakespeare was the first existentialist, while others claim Søren Kierkegaard (1813–1855) was the father of existentialism. As evidenced by these variations, existentialism is hard to pin down, has multiple definitions, can be fragmented, and contains various strains within its own movement. Finding the logical and universal hierarchies of Kant and Hegel suspect, existentialists were precursors to the "postmodern" movement (see chapter 12). In fact, existentialists believe that reason was inadequate to discovering transcendent truths; they prefer the subjective to the objective, perception to objectivity.

At base, *existentialism is a philosophy of existence*. It studies how we exist, why we exist, and suggests new ways to live our lives. Instead of starting with objects, as do empiricists and sensualists, it starts with the study of the subject—the who, the person who lives everyday. To this mix, the existentialists add certain principles that help further define their revolt against the modern rationalists. Existentialists believe that we are free to choose as opposed to being determined by a preset causation. In fact, we are condemned to freedom; we have no choice but to choose. We are defined by the choices we make and we develop our sense of self in making choices. Thus, freedom leads to a sense of self and to growth, but we are also responsible for the choices we make. Taking responsibility for what we do and what we decide is living an "authentic" existence.

Kierkegaard (1813–1855)

The earliest existential philosopher was born in Copenhagen on May 5, 1813. A contemporary of the influential Hegel, Søren Kierkegaard attempted to refute Hegel's dialectical certitude and theory of historic progress by arguing that "All essential knowledge relates to existence." His small inheritance allowed him to attend the University of Copenhagen and to devote his life to writing. His call for an authentic Christianity got him branded as a heretic and fanatic. His last major work, *Attack on "Christendom,"* was published in the year of his death; it satirized the state church of Denmark. Although he was ridiculed in his own time, his writings eventually proved enormously influential in the twentieth century, particularly following the horrors of the world wars, which badly undermined the optimism of the modernists.

One of the great quests of existentialism is "the transcendent," which has at least two meanings. Earlier we touched on the first—to transcend means to rise above. For example, if you are involved in a dispute in which it is posited that you either favor or oppose affirmative action, you can transcend the argument by showing that you are neither for nor against it. Kierkegaard used this rising-above method to transcend Hegel's dialectical scheme, arguing that there was a legitimate position beyond the thesis and anti-thesis. Kierkegaard endorsed the One (primordial unity) over the dialectical duality of Hegel's logic. Remember that Hegel and Kant endorsed material experience as reality; to be an experience, something or some phenomenon had to be separated from something else. Hence, an automatic division or dialectic is inherent in Hegel's system. For Kierkegaard, however, consciousness itself transcends these divisions as a reflection of the One. The One transcends the material of experience; consciousness presides over and is superior to the collision between ideality and reality. For Kierkegaard, then, consciousness is a reflection of the One in that consciousness allows the growth of self in this transcendence of experience. That realization is a freeing moment which allows the self to control its own destiny. Like Socrates, he argued that "one must know oneself before knowing anything else." He is considered the father of existentialism, at least in part because he made the subject the proper study of philosophy. His path is the path of subjectivity: "One does not become a hero or a lover objectively." The self should not be objectified because although it is always existing in a "mode," it is not always existing in the same "mode." It is not static, but constantly changing as it makes decisions.

A second meaning of transcendent is spirit, that which allows access to God. Kierkegaard believed that the self contains spirit—that in a sense we are all divine. Only when the self raises the question of existence for itself and experiences it as an existing being in the world, can it transcend the everyday categorization of self and find its spiritual nature, which will lead to transcendent Spirit, that is, God. George Bedell writes that for Kierkegaard

> the Spirit is, above all else, an infinitely powerful spirit, absolutely transcendent to the world, who breaks open the contained and orderly Greek cosmos. Therefore, Spirit, who in the final analysis is God, is not beauty and truth but energy and power. . . . He does not simply inspire poets or warriors as in the Greek world; He is the very foundation of freedom to be or to choose one's existence.

But how do we find "self"? How does the "mode" we choose contribute to the search? There are at least two ways to find the self. First, we need to consider self as a subject-actor in an experiential world and examine who or what is making choices—who or what is relating to others. We live every moment of our existence by choosing. Decision making reveals being, because being *is* decision making. Kierkegaard wrote that "in making a choice it is not so much a question of choosing the right as of the energy, the earnestness, the pathos with which one chooses." In his *Concluding Unscientific Postscript*, he reasserted this position when he claimed that it is not *what* a person decides but ***how*** one decides, because how a person decides defines self. Our decisions reveal our *ethos*; how we make decisions is determined by ***who*** we are, inclusive of our values.

The question of values leads to the second means of self-discovery. Since values serve as guides in decision making, we need to know our core values or we will continue to act in the dark, out of ignorance. Such knowledge comes from intense self-examination and reflection. Kierkegaard concluded that the subject acts, perceives, and defines the world; this creative capacity is what gives us a sense of "selfhood." That self becomes "authentic" *when it takes responsibility for the decisions it makes.*

The existential path to authenticity runs through three stages or "modes of life": *the aesthetic*, which Kierkegaard defined as immediate and unreflective; *the ethical*, which he defined as reflective in the sense that we examine values in a rational, moral way; and *the religious*, which he defined as spiritual or devoted.

The aesthetic stage in life is reactive; for many people, it is all there is and they never rise above it. Such people are not in control of their lives because they are reactive; their behavior is determined by others. Existentialists claim that if you begin to reflect on your life, you will begin to see that the aesthetic life will always let you down; it will eventually disappoint you. This understanding can, as Kierkegaard makes clear, lead to a paralysis of the will, a tremendous sense of indifference to the world and to those who populate it.

One is shaken from this apathy in unique ways. For example, you can fall into depression, what Kierkegaard called "melancholia." While depressed, you might perform some demonic act, being cruel to a beggar, kicking a cat, or uttering a mean remark. When you commit such acts, you should have the revelation that they are not you; that the "you in you" would not act in such a way. This "dread" can break through your indifference. You are suddenly shaken from your apathy in an effort to restore a sense of self. It is that effort that leads to the ethical stage. For example, when some alcoholics hit bottom, they vow to change their existence. The glutton catches a reflection in the mirror that awakens him or her to the emptiness of his or her existence. Pain lets us know we are alive, and glimpses of our inauthentic existences lead us to seek an authentic sense of ourselves.

The ethical life is difficult because it requires reflection and a re-prioritizing of values, our guides to decision making. It requires that we find and chose to embrace the authentic sense of self. Most existentialists spend a good deal of time on the question of guilt. It is closely linked to discovering a sense of self, to the values we hold, and to the issue of responsibility. Guilt can arise because we are overwhelmed by the choices we have available. Whatever choice we make, we will decide against something and for something else. Deciding against causes us to feel guilty.

Guilt also arises when we violate our values. Here the voice of conscience reminds us that we have been offending the guides that we claim to follow. We are drinking or eating to excess—and harming ourselves and others in the process. In this case, we must either redefine the values we embrace (a conscious act of choice and re-creation of self) or we must admit to having committed a sin and take responsibility for such action in an effort to improve (a reaffirmation of self). In Dostoyevsky's *Crime and Punishment*, Raskolnikoff commits a senseless murder of an elderly woman, surely a demonic act. He wrestles with his conscience, a process which he soon learns is worse than torture and imprisonment. The important thing to note is that *something feels the guilt, and that something is the authentic person inside us.* According to existentialists, until we go through such trauma, we remain a mystery to ourselves—incapable of leading authentic lives, let alone transcending to spirit. Thus, while the end goal of existentialism is self-affirming and spiritual, the path to that goal is often dark and troubling.

The last stage in Kierkegaard's project of life, the religious, brings us intuitive knowledge of a transcendent God. R. G. Collingwood puts it this way: "[M]an is also the being whose being is to transcend himself. To the extent to which he submits his will to the will of God he overcomes his self-alienation and fulfills the conditions of his inherent rationality." Transcendence is difficult because the grammar and logic of ordinary mind (GLOOM) is committed to keeping us in the experiential, material world. Its vocabulary is inadequate for a world outside the universe or inside our souls. For example, what does Kierkegaard mean when he says that the individual is an "existing infinite spirit"? Existing is temporal, real, contingent; existing is also an abstract concept; finally, existence is decisive actualization. It is this actualizing by reflective decision that Kierkegaard implores us to embrace. When the self relates its existence to itself, it exists spiritually: "*Spirit's realization as self-consciousness is, then, the initial effort of the self to relate itself to itself.*" Spirit arises from creating a sense of self. Freedom to discover and experiment with self is crucial to the process. Freedom creates infinite possibilities and frees the self from being locked into necessity, that is, concrete, pre-determined, and/or factual limits. Freedom allows the play of the "either/or," and in choosing we develop selfhood.

In Kierkegaard's work we see the first glimpses of what existentialism might contribute to rhetorical theory. A Kierkegaardian would employ rhetoric *to force and make choices which would manifest self-knowledge, providing a more secure presence for the leap to transcendence.* Rhetoric creates self because speakers make choices as they compose and deliver speeches, and they bring choices to their audiences, who also can use them to assert selfhood. The presence of that self is a means to transcendence and the self is revealed in authentic decision making—taking responsibility for what we choose.

The subjective world of Kierkegaard was full of implicit rhetorical theory concerning responsibility. For example, a person breaks with the thoughtless immediacy of the aesthetic life by ending gossip and other useless forms of communication. On the positive side, Kierkegaard specifically called for "edifying discourse," which helps redefine self in an authentic way by accepting free choice and responsibility for existence. Unfortunately for those trying to build a theory of responsible communication, Kierkegaard claimed that "edifying discourse" cannot be communicated by lecturing, arguing, or persuading. Kierkegaard's denigration of public or direct rhetoric leads him to endorse an indirect approach. Edifying discourse is glimpsed in art or seen in a telling example; it is seductive and often ambiguous. The reason for this indirection is that direct appeals, according to Kierkegaard, fail to liberate the person addressed from the illusions of the aesthetic stage of life. In *Point of View of the Author*, he wrote:

> [A]n illusion can never be destroyed directly . . . only by indirect means can it be radically removed. . . . A direct attack only strengthens a person in his illusions, and at the same time embitters him. . . . This is what is achieved by the indirect method which . . . arranges everything dialectically for the prospective captive, and then shyly withdraws . . . so as not to witness the admission which he makes to himself alone before God—that he has lived hitherto in an illusion.

How do we *practice* indirect communication for the good of us or another person; that is, how do we use language to help ourselves and others destroy the illusions of the inauthentic life (such as money and power) and embrace an authentic sense of self—a self that is free to choose, a self that accepts responsibility for choice, and a self that uses its freedom creatively to reinforce its individuality?

Kierkegaard cited the use of ambiguity as an example of indirect communication. His endorsement of ambiguity arose from his notion of faith. Kierkegaard argued that if God had saved Jesus from the cross, he would have made faith impossible because disbelief would be impossible. Thus, uncertainty is crucial to producing faith. Ambiguity promotes uncertainty. Kierkegaard saw it as a means of teaching others because it arouses attention and it forces choices. If the ambiguity is artfully constructed, it will force us to choose and in choosing we exercise the self.

For Kierkegaard and most of the other existentialists authenticity leads to *commitment*—living the life you recommend. In rhetorical theory, this means practicing what you preach. In philosophy, it means exemplifying what you advise. Socrates did both. He recommended the contemplative life to his pupils and led that life. He was committed to it and, therefore, projected a sense of authenticity. Had he become a politician, he would have demonstrated a lack of commitment to what he preached. Thus, a Kierkegaardian notion of *ethos* would include holding speakers responsible for exemplifying their messages.

Sartre (1905–1980)

As an atheist, Jean Paul Sartre would dispute being connected with anything as other-worldly as spirit, but he clearly strengthened the role freedom plays in the authentic life and further eroded confidence in objective reason. Sartre argued in *Being and Nothingness* that consciousness "is free by virtue of its being aware of its possibilities, of what it lacks, or of its privations." In fact, persons are "condemned" to freedom: we have no choice but to decide. Even when we do not decide, we have made the decision not to act. So how do we make a *responsible* decision? In *Existentialism and Humanism*, Sartre attempted to provide an answer: "And, when we say that man is responsible for himself, we do not mean that he is responsible only for his individuality, but that he is responsible for all men."

In his investigation of responsibility, Sartre, like Kierkegaard, revealed the importance of the creative use of language. He claimed that if self-persuasion was powerful enough to be used for inauthentic purposes, what he called "bad faith" or "self-deception," then it could also be used creatively to embrace freedom, discover the self, and remake existence. "Man is nothing else but that which he makes himself. . . . You are free, therefore choose—that is to say invent." In this way, a Sartrean might endorse a speaker's creative use of language to demonstrate a sense of self.

Sartre helped popularize existentialism in the post-World War II era by writing clearly on the subject, by representing its themes in novels and plays, and by bringing credibility to the movement since he had been a member of the French resistance during World War II. His notoriety was enhanced when in 1948 he was condemned by both the Communist Party and the Catholic church. His life-long liaison with the novelist and early feminist Simone de Beauvoir, and his habit of discussing his philosophy in the coffee houses on the Left Bank in Paris, did nothing to diminish his fame.

One of Sartre's clearest injunctions is that "existence precedes essence," by which he meant that self comes before anything masks it. In his novel *Nausea*, Sartre explained that existence has no connection with "assigned essence." Persons are beings prior to being covered over by what others attribute to their class. In this case, the term essence refers to the historic fragrances that arise from the qualities a person is assigned by society. These fragrances, to mix a metaphor, blind persons to their being and blind a person to the authentic existence of others. In *Existentialism and Humanism*, Sartre provided a case in point when he railed against the generalizations that have been made about existentialists by Communists, Christians, and others. He concluded, "So it appears that ugliness is being identified with existentialism." That is, the authentic pre-existing existential philosophy has been covered over by the historic slanders of its enemies. These slanders have become its "essence," which in this case is an odor that prejudices the public against it.

The operation of racism provides a case in our own time. Elements in a society sometimes attribute characteristics to a race and assume that each member of the race possesses those characteristics. Persons born into that race are sometimes blinded to their own individuality and assume the characteristics attributed to them, bowing to the authority of society or accepting a past not of their own making. Appearing before a Senate committee studying the plight of blacks in the armed forces, former Secretary of the Army Clifford Alexander said:

> White America continues to paint pictures of black America that determine our opportunities. You see us as less than you are. You think that we are not as smart, not as energetic, not as well suited to supervise you. . . . These are the ways you perceive us, and your perceptions are negative. They are fed by motion pictures, ad agencies, news people and television.

Alexander believes society has covered blacks with disfiguring essences that prevent them from reaching their potential.

Existentialists seek to break through these undifferentiated perceptions by dispelling the "assigned essences" and allowing the individual being to emerge. While Sartre cautioned against accepting "assigned essences," he encouraged his followers to find their own sense of "Being-in-itself" to create an authentic essence. Basically, he argued that existence was unconscious, and that in arriving at one's authentic self, one becomes conscious of "Being-in-itself," one's true essence for operating in the world.

Why should we undertake such a project? Because the alternative is assigned essence, which is a form of stereotyping. Existentialists believe that stereotyping is wrong for at least two reasons. First, it does not represent persons as they really are; it objectifies them. However, according to existentialists, human beings do not exist in static categories; they are always becoming or "on the way" to becoming something. This fluid state presents us with a stream of decisions; life's potential is not bound up in the categories we inherit or those created by logicians; it is free flowing and hence open to creative forces.

Second, stereotyping prevents persons from realizing their potential to create a self. This covering over of being retards development and leads to artificial understandings of self. The woman with the potential to become a doctor becomes a disappointed housewife instead because she buys into the subculture's characterization of women in general. In such cases, the individual loses a sense of "mineness" and control over one's activities, one's existence. The danger is that if society determines what we do with our lives, it determines who we are.

Central to this analysis is the notion of underlying being or an "authentic" self. Philosophers of existence, as we have seen, get at this concept by emphasizing human experience from the perspective of the subject, as opposed to treating humans as objects to be analyzed. Instead of a scientific or analytic approach to the question of self, the existentialists take a phenomenological approach. That is, they examine existence in context and as a whole without imposing the presuppositions of previous philosophical speculation. Situating his study on the realities of existence prompted Sartre's "revolt against both abstract reason and scientific determinism." He was clearly a postmodern thinker.

Earlier we noted that Sartre strengthened the role freedom has to play in the authentic life. Here we should also note that feedom overwhelms the individual with choices and may cause anxiety. Anxiety in turn leads to a crisis which, according to Sartre, can have either authentic or inauthentic consequences. The inauthentic person will try to flee the crisis by re-immersing into the herd mentality of the world. The authentic person will embrace the crisis, which will lead to two further reactions: The person will be thrown back upon his or her self, which will lead to intense self-examination; or the person will reach out for communion with others, which may lead to a discovery of self-with-others. In both cases, authenticity arises from the realization that our absolute freedom means we are "absolutely responsible" not only for our decisions but for the situations in which we find ourselves.

If we have no choice but to decide, and we dare not let others make our choices for us, what guidelines do we use? Sartre responded that "nothing can be good for us without being good for all." Humans must decide as if they were deciding for all humankind. This advice leads to a tension between freedom and responsibility in the works of Sartre. He faced this dilemma: pure freedom cannot be responsible because of the damage it does to others, and anything short of freedom is dangerous because of the damage it can do to the development of the self. Sartre's discussion of the immorality of marriage proves enlightening on this point. If a husband is totally free, he will make his wife into a slave, which is evil. If the husband treats his wife as an equal, then neither are totally free, which is damaging to the development of the potential of each. If the husband gives his wife total freedom, he becomes a slave. If the husband is indifferent to the situation, he is inauthentic, because he is no husband at all while frozen in the ice of his own indifference. There is "no exit" except to transcend the situation by deciding and taking responsibility for the awful choice.

One of Sartre's early attempts to escape this bind came in personal experience. For him, freedom was essential to authentic existence, and it could be found even in the most desperate situations if one could transcend them. He determined that we are always free to assert our sense of self and that is the most important freedom. In *The Republic of Silence*, he explained:

> We were never more free than during the German occupation. We had lost all our rights, beginning with the right to talk. Every day we were insulted to our faces and had to take it in silence. Under one pretext or another, as workers, Jews, or political prisoners, we were deported *en masse*. . . . And because of all this we were free. Because the Nazi venom seeped into our thoughts, every accurate thought was a conquest. Because an all-powerful police tried to force us to hold our tongues, every word took on the value of a declaration of principles. Because we were hunted down, every one of our gestures had the weight of a solemn commitment. . . . And the choice that each of us made of his life was an authentic choice because it was made face to face with death, because it could always have been expressed in these terms: "Rather death than . . ." And here I am not speaking of the elite among us who were real Resistants, but of all Frenchmen who, at every hour of night and day throughout four years, answered *No*.

Here we learn that even in the face of annihilation, we can save our selves. We assert the self by saying "no." This discovery led Sartre to see that non-being is a permanent possibility and a reinforcement of authentic being. Nothingness haunts, inspires, and defines being. In such a world, invention is critical; that is, we must not accept what is thrust upon us, instead we must take responsibility for our own personal freedom since we are what we do in the world. This step will result in an authentic sense of selfhood and, for Sartre, the "good of all."

One of the most fascinating characteristics of Sartre's thinking is that it converts the negative to the positive: nothingness helps define being; that we have no exit demonstrates that we have freedom. He used a similar strategy when he advanced his theory of rhetoric. He began by talking about how rhetoric can be used for self-deceit in chapter 2, "Bad Faith" in *Being and Nothingness*. His point is that individuals often try to escape the responsible freedom of being-for-itself (*être-pour-soi*) by committing a "lie in the soul." This violation of conscience is maintained through such rhetorical strategies as role playing, diminishing, rationalizing, sublimating, emphasizing, or avoiding certain "facts." Sartre understood that these rhetorical strategies could cover the truth and delude the self.

Since Sartre would have us re-create our selves authentically—that is, without deception and stripped of acquired essences—he provided a basic rationale for an intrapersonal communication. We must speak to ourselves in inventive ways that help free us from controlling and covering essences, categories, assessments and the like. Furthermore, because what we decide and what we "fashion" is done for all humankind, public persuasion must endorse what is good for all of us.

Heidegger (1889–1976)

Like Kierkegaard, Martin Heidegger believed that we cannot find transcendent "Being" until we affirm the "being" in ourselves. Once we realize that we are beings-in-the-world (*da-sein* as he called it), we are in a position to see that we reflect transcendent Being. Heidegger's theory is linked to rhetoric in several ways, the most important of which is his claim that language is the "house of Being" and can lead us to transcendent truths, even dark ones. For Heidegger, truth was "un-concealment" (*a-letheia*). Heidegger sought to free the individual first from the "leveling" influence of the "they" (the common mob or herd) and then from the rational conventions of Aristotle, Descartes, Hegel, and Kant, because their systems were inimical to the "poetizing thought" of the mystical side of being that leads to the transcendent, "the great poem speaking us into being."

Heidegger, who was born in Germany, became a Jesuit novice and attended the University of Freiburg, where he became a teacher and eventually rector. When he studied with Edmund Husserl (as did Sartre), Heidegger became fascinated with his teacher's philosophy of phenomenology, which claimed to examine the world from a presuppositionless point of view. Husserl's famous motto was "to the things themselves." By 1927, however, Heidegger found inadequacies in Husserl's theory, particularly when it came to interpreting phenomena. In response, Heidegger invented hermeneutic phenomenology to replace it. As we have seen, hermeneutic means a close reading under watchful observation to provide an interpretation that discovers the authentic meaning of a text. Phenomenology attempts to see things in material context—as they are in the whole without being subject to the scalpel of analytic logic or scientific dissection. Phenomenologists argue that we should experience phenomena without presuppositions, biases, or predetermined filters. They want us to see the forest as it is, not as what someone has told us a forest should be, and not as the trees into which the scientists would divide the forest. They want us to see trees as they are, not as leaves and bark; a tree is poetic until broken into its scientific parts. In a way, Heidegger provided the best of both worlds with his hermeneutic phenomenology: he insured close observation by using hermeneutics and he insured that the larger picture would contextualize phenomena without distortion by using phenomenology. In the process of applying his new methodology, he took many positions inspired by Kierkegaard, whom he often cites.

During his tenure as Rector of Freiburg, Heidegger gave an address in 1934 endorsing the platform of the National Socialist (Nazi) Party. Although Heidegger later claimed he was "not a Nazi," and although he helped Jewish professors escape Nazi Germany, his early and brief support of Hitler left him tarred in the eyes of many and raised the question of responsibility in existential philosophy, a question to which we will return in a few pages. In any case, Heidegger retired into Germany's Black Forest in 1959 and lived a reclusive life with his wife. Nonetheless his writings became enormously influential; in fact, in the fifties there were more chairs of Heideggerian philosophy in Europe than those named for any other philosopher.

In his landmark work of 1927, *Being and Time*, Heidegger opposed using the term *spirit* (*Geist*) because many of the definitions of spirit provided by prior philosophers had "thingified" it. For example, when Hegel referred to history as essentially the history of spirit, he meant an unfolding of a cultural tradition on the road to freedom; but to Heidegger this was much too material. As Jacques Derrida, the contemporary deconstructionist, makes clear, "The Hegelian determination of spirit remains ordered, prescribed, ruled by the epoch of the

Cartesian *cogito*." Instead, Heidegger believed that spirit "is what in no way allows itself to be thingified." Its power "unites and engages, assigns, obliges." Spirituality is having and demonstrating transcendent truth. Associating with spirit always expands consciousness and does so exponentially.

To what do existentialists refer when they write about spirit? Spirit concerns other-worldly goodness and an inner sense, often associated with grace. Spirit is a matter of faith and/or intuition which sets an example; it is not a matter of reason or objectivity. It may inspire outward wisdom, as in the story of Solomon moved by the "spirit of wisdom," but it is mainly ethereal, incorporeal, invisible, and not measurable by objective standards. Aldus Huxley, the English writer, explained why when he wrote, "[M]an possesses a double nature, a phenomenal ego and an eternal Self, which is the inner man, the spirit, the spark of divinity within the soul."

To find spirit, Heidegger said that humans must first understand that presence is the experience of existence; the I thinking precedes all other presences and the experience of all other beings. In this way, Heidegger reflected the thinking of Descartes. Individuals thinking is what is most present and that thinking process comes before any other experience. Individuals have to be conscious before they can be conscious of something. Heidegger wanted us to closely examine this conscious state to establish our "being," much in the way that Sartre wanted us to understand that existence precedes essence.

Heidegger then urged humans to let go of the established ground; thinking must follow the path a free language opens. However, finding the play of Being in language is not enough. Heidegger claimed humans have to be ready to receive spirit; the person must stand in "harkening attunement" detached from the distractions of this world. Only then will the voice of Being come to us. Thus, *authentic listening*, another component of existential rhetorical theory, is crucial to attaining existential spirituality.

Once transcendence has been experienced, Heidegger argued that it was possible to bring that experience to others by using his version of authentic rhetoric: "poetizing" in constructive and creative ways. By poetizing, Heidegger did not mean writing or speaking poetry—he meant thinking and speaking in inventive ways that uncover and reveal the transcendent truth. The inventive process means giving one's self over to the alien, to the dark, and to wandering in the open, exposed. When conjoined with a concerned harkening, authentic discourse allows the emergence of *logos*, the voice of Being. Then a person may choose to move through the threshold of Being into a dialogue of transcendent quality, which would uncover truth. Heidegger left his readers with the promise that transcendence is there if only one works diligently enough to achieve it. Such a rhetoric would sever individuals from the "they," avoid gossip, situate individuals in harkening attunement, and develop ways to bring others to Being by using the making-known and constructive functions of rhetoric. Heidegger recommended three such forms as "authentic": (1) the examination of language to discover the self as already in the world (*Befindlichkeit*), (2) the use of language to uncover the truth (*Verstehen*), and (3) meaningful discourse (*Rede*). Each of these has a corresponding "inauthentic" form: (1) the use of ambiguous language (*Zeideutigkiet*), (2) distracting curiosity (*Neugier*), and (3) idle chatter, gossip, or prattle (*Gerede*). Heidegger, then, posited a rhetorical theory that moved from inauthentic interpersonal chatter to authentic intrapersonal dialogue with Being.

Jaspers (1883–1969) and Buber (1878–1965)

To this point, we have examined six markers on the path to spirit: rejection of the herd mentality, creative use of language, examination of self, concerned listening, accepting responsibility for decisions, and freedom to choose. All are influential on the road recommended by Karl Jaspers and Martin Buber, who situated these elements in authentic interpersonal relationships. Rejecting the solipsism of Kierkegaard and the atheism of Sartre, Jaspers (a Catholic) and Buber (a Jewish rabbi) emphasized that dialectical reciprocity can lead to an authentic sense of self and others. Jaspers was a German psychologist who became a philosopher; his writing is dense and full of evidence. Buber was a Jewish theologian whose approach is poetic.

Heidegger laid some groundwork for Buber and Jaspers when he pointed out that "The mode of being of language is talk among human beings. It is constitutive of being-with-one-another, that is, constitutive of human sociality." Yet more important to our purposes, he pointed out that "Hearing is constitutive for discourse." While speaking can be monological, hearing requires dialogue. You listen to an other, not to nothing, even if the other is your inner voice or the voice of conscience.

Jaspers and Buber described an authentic dialogic as the rhetoric of response (I-Thou) as distinguished from a monological rhetoric of isolation (I-it). The dialogic relationship encourages each partner to identify the potential for authentic existence in the other. Said Jaspers, "Self-being is only real in communication with another self-being." It is one of the choices we can make; and for Jaspers, "Self-understanding begins with the individual concrete acts of choice." The formulation prescribed goes through several steps including the discovery of self as recommended by Kierkegaard, the discovery of another authentic person with whom to have free and open dialogue in pursuit of further authentic understandings, and the realization of the transcendent *in* the relationship.

Jaspers and Buber emphasized that *dialectical reciprocity* can help infuse a sense of responsibility. For Buber, communication in I-Thou relationships is characterized as immediate, confrontational, risky, direct, exclusive, creative, responsible, unfolding, and confirming. For Jaspers, "It involves complete openness, unqualified renunciation of the uses of power and advantage, and concerns the other's self-realization as fully one's own." In such relationships, the subjective I has power, acts, and—very importantly—invents creatively. In inauthentic relationships, the I and/or the other is objective; that is, passive, acted upon, and incapable of creativity.

Dialogue that is open and empathetic is more likely to confirm a sense of self in the other person because it is less distracted than other forms of communication. Public speakers are concerned with their messages; shoppers are concerned with the product and its price. However, people in dialogue are more concerned with issues of self than people at work or play. Dialogue breaks down presuppositions and causes each person to be preoccupied with the being of the other.

Like Heidegger and Kierkegaard, Buber and Jaspers also see the transcendent as inspirational of art. That is, all of them believe that true art reflects a glimpse of the transcendent. Buber and Jaspers, however, define the transcendent in an interpersonal way. It is the manifestation of a sense of self, the construction of self through the use of creative language in a dialogue, and a higher sense of self developed in cooperation with another away from the leveling masses. Jaspers saw the desire for conformity as a terrible enemy: "In nonexistential mundane existence, the decisive factor is the leveling will of nonentities."

THE EXISTENTIAL CHALLENGE

We have explored the reaction of five existentialists to the modernism of Hegel and Kant. These philosophers of existence can help us understand how individuals retrieve spirit and achieve transcendence. They demonstrate that freedom allows for the creative use of language which in turn leads to a sense of self and possibly association with the transcendent. They challenge us to reconstruct life in such a way as to make each of us the captain of our destiny. If the existentialists are correct, then creative use of language can serve both individuals and society. It can provide the strategies for the authentic reconstitution of self. It can provide the ambiguity for the indirect persuasion of Kierkegaard's "edifying discourse." It can provide such strategies as minimization and rationalization for Sartre's invention of self and the freedom in language that would help those engaged in I-Thou relationships.

That brings us back to the nettlesome question of responsibility. What is the existential theory of conscience? Consistently, those who have written about the existential roots of spirituality have faced the argument that existentialism can be used to justify the rhetoric of a Louis Farrakhan as well as a Martin Luther King, Jr. There are two problems here. First, the existentialists, like the Platonists before them, are right to point out that sometimes rhetorical transactions promote evil. Murray Edelman cites an interesting case from recent American history:

> *The Pentagon Papers* show that the intelligent, highly educated policy makers of the Kennedy and Johnson Administrations were convinced that military intervention in Vietnam would stop the spread of world communism through a war that would be won quickly at small cost, and that they continued to believe it after several years of counter-evidence—exemplifying a degree of reconstruction of reality few psychotics can ever have matched.

Edelman's example reinforces Sartre's point: our minds are so powerful when it comes to language that we can fool ourselves. For this reason, existentialists are rightly sensitive to the charge that their subjective approach can invite irresponsible action. We know that talent in public speaking does not always serve the good. We must not be afraid to issue ethical judgments that protect the community and ourselves from the irresponsible actions of orators and audiences. To be credible, such ethical assessments must be grounded in philosophies which *hold individuals accountable for the choices they make.* Existentialism provides such a philosophy.

That leads to the second problem with existential notions of responsibility. Since existentialists often seek to transcend worldly questions by focusing on *how* decisions are made instead of *what* they are, their critics often ask, what constitutes the correct/moral use of authenticity? Can't persons who believe they have a clear understanding of self, who have made a leap of faith, and who take responsibility for their actions, still commit evil acts? Existentialists answer this challenge by making each of us accountable for our decisions. This call for personal responsibility constitutes a safeguard against irresponsible action. However, different existentialists provide different measures of responsibility.

A stronger safety net might be built by combining the various injunctions of the existentialists into an eight-part test useful to our quest. Synthesizing the existentialists we have examined in this chapter, we can deduce the following questions to establish a foundation for authenticity and responsibility in rhetorical transactions:

1. What evidence exists that the speaker has subjected values to scrutiny and has a clear, undeceived understanding of self?
2. Does the speaker take responsibility for the speech and the action it advocates?
3. Does the speaker encourage audience members to make decisions and take responsibility for them?
4. What evidence exists to demonstrate that the speaker has engaged in authentic dialogue as a check against solipsism and as a means of reinforcing a sense of self?
5. What evidence exists that the speaker has reached conclusions by deciding as if he/she were deciding for all of humankind?
6. What evidence exists that the speaker has moved beyond immediate gratification to stages of moral and ethical development?
7. What evidence exists that the speaker heard the call of conscience or was inspired by transcendent spirit?
8. What evidence exists that the speaker is committed to what is recommended?

If used properly these means of accountability should help reveal whether a speaker was responsible and hence contributed to authenticity among listeners.

CONCLUSION

Our examination of existential rhetoric has led to a theory of creativity: since the manipulation of language forces choice, it helps us develop a sense of self which in turn allows us to associate with spirit. If we can associate with spirit, we can use that association to refine our rhetoric, to make it more artistic. Furthermore, rhetoric is a creative art form that calls others to the transcendent level. What the philosophers examined in this chapter contribute to this formulation is *the way to spirit*; what rhetoric provides is an *art form by which spirit can be expressed and by which others can be brought to a sense of it*. If, as some believe, spirit is the call of conscience, then rhetoric is a way by which speakers can make that call known to others. From the prophets of old to the moral politicians of the twentieth century, rhetoric has been used in the service of conscience.

Mahatma Gandhi provides a clear example. Gandhi was able to move masses with his gentle speech and his devotion to nonviolence. For many, Gandhi was a living saint who inspired a nation. By fasting, he brought a national civil war to a halt from his sickbed. Socrates was enormously influential in much smaller settings where inhibitions were reduced (usually with wine), where he was involved in a one-on-one dialogue, and where those present seemed interested in pursuing and sharing knowledge in an environment of mutual respect.

Whereas the pursuit of spirit is certainly the province of religion, it is not *solely* the province of religion as the several approaches of the five existential philosophers suggest. Great rhetoric exemplifies a means to retrieval of spirit: creating with language. Like the palette of the painter or the notes of the musician, words provide the substance of the rhetor's art. Even these comparisons do not give language its due, because it can be more subtle than any hue a painter can produce and has much more variety than the combination of notes available to the composer. Language is the stuff of an ultimate art which is better able than any other to help us reach a sense of spirit through creativity and to hear the call of conscience through its making-known function.

Rhetoric has a role to play in the existential project. As an art form, it can reveal freedom, force choices, and call others to spirit. It can question, use, and prioritize values, which serve as guides for the self. It can, by quieting itself, establish an attitude of "harkening attunement" to spirit. It can provide the creative dialogue of authentic "I-Thou" relationships. In short, rhetoric provides a *praxis*, a practical operation for existentialism which copes with the provisional nature of knowledge and the uncertainty of everyday existence. Existentialism provides a measure of authenticity that enhances the responsible use of rhetoric. It is hard to imagine a happier marriage of disciplines.

Section Twelve: Meaning

SECTION TWELVE
Meaning

Timothy Borchers

The study of meaning is often traced to two British theorists, Charles Kay (C. K.) Ogden and I. A. Richards (1928). You can read more about them in Box 5.1. Their book, *The Meaning of Meaning*, is the prime source for understanding their theory of language. Ogden and Richards were some of the first theorists interested in how language led to miscommunication and how it could be used more effectively. Their focus was on the "fundamental characteristics of language" (Condit, 1995, p. 214). Ogden and Richards "hoped that if individuals knew the likely pitfalls of language, they could speak more accurately and thereby communicate more effectively" (Condit, 1995, p. 214). In a series of lectures at Bryn Mawr College in 1936, Richards defined rhetoric as "a study of misunderstanding and its remedies" (1936, p. 3). He explained further, "We struggle all our days with misunderstandings, and no apology is required for any study which can prevent or remove them" (p. 3).

Richards argued that it was important to focus on the language of rhetoric in its own right. We could not, he explained, focus simply on the thoughts, ideas, or "bare notions" about which language discusses. Richards (1936) explained, "The trouble is that we *can* only 'collect the whole sum and tenor of the discourse' from the words, we cannot 'lay aside the words'; and as to considering 'the bare notions themselves'" (p. 5). Richards was reacting to thinking similar to that of Plato, who wanted to separate the words used in rhetoric from the "true" thoughts the words expressed. For Richards, the words were part of the equation and ideas could not be studied apart from the language through which they were expressed. Thus, a study of language and meaning was necessary to understanding rhetoric.

An important aspect of his and Ogden's work was Basic English, an 850-word vocabulary of English words that they believed could be used by anyone in any situation to communicate clearly. By using only a few, clearly defined words, it was thought that people could more easily reach understanding. Richards spent time in China teaching Basic English while Ogden founded the Orthological Institute to promote the spread of Basic English. British prime ministers Neville Chamberlain and Winston Churchill, who provided government funding for the project, supported the movement. A list of the 850 words in Basic English is available at http://ogden.basic-english.org/words.html. Despite their efforts, Basic English never really gained popularity, and it lost government support in Great Britain when Churchill left office in 1945.

BOX 5.1 Biography of a Theorist: Ogden and Richards

Charles Ogden was born June 1, 1889. As an undergraduate at Cambridge University, he was interested in the study of language and would become an author, editor, and translator later in life. I. A. Richards was born on February 26, 1893 in Cheshire, England. Like Ogden, he studied at Cambridge University. Richards was interested in history and philosophy and planned to become a psychoanalyst.

In 1918, Ogden and Richards began work on *The Meaning of Meaning*, which was published in a series of journal articles. In 1923, the work was published as a book. They also developed the theory of Basic English—a limited set of words that should be used in order to reduce confusion. Ogden worked for a variety of publications and continued to promote the study of Basic English. Richards held a variety of academic positions and continued to collaborate with Ogden on several additional works. In 1939, Richards came to the United States to teach at Harvard University, where he developed textbooks to help teach Basic English. Ogden died on March 21, 1957; Richards lived until Sept. 7, 1979.

The Semantic Triangle

We can begin to understand Ogden and Richards' view of meaning by studying their concept of the **semantic triangle** (Figure 5.1). The semantic triangle outlines the relationship between the three elements of meaning: symbols (words or

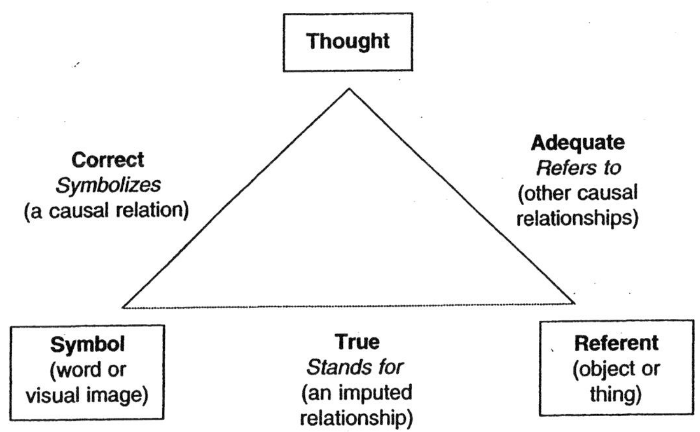

FIGURE 5.1 Semantic Triangle.

Adapted from C. K. Ogden and I. A. Richards, *The Meaning of Meaning* (New York: Harcourt, Brace, and Company, 1923). Author rendering.

images), thoughts (the ideas we have about symbols), and referents (the objects referred to by symbols). By understanding the relationship between these elements, we can better understand Ogden and Richards' theory of meaning.

Ogden and Richards (1928) explained that symbols cause certain thoughts, and, reciprocally, certain thoughts cause the use of certain symbols. Thus, the relationship between symbols and thoughts is causal in nature. They explained that

"When we speak, the symbolism we employ is caused partly by the reference we are making and partly by social and psychological factors—the purpose for which we are making the reference, the proposed effect of our symbols on other persons, and our own attitude" (pp. 10–11). That is, if you are to persuade someone, you are likely to use particular symbols to do so. Your intent causes you to use one symbol over another. Likewise, if you are nervous in a communication situation, your symbol use may be affected. Your nervousness and uncertainty may cause you to say particular words.

Conversely, when we are the receiver, our thoughts are caused by the symbols others communicate to us. Ogden and Richards (1928) explained, "When we hear what is said, the symbols both cause us to perform an act of reference and to assume an attitude" (p. 11). When you see a car commercial on television, for instance, you might recall a similar feeling of freedom and escape depicted in the commercial. Or, when a politician appeals for your vote, he or she may say something that causes you to support their candidacy.

On the other side of the triangle in Figure 5.1, there is a similar type of relationship. When we physically see the referent, such as the book you are reading or the chair in which you are sitting, we think of that book or chair or you can think of objects, or referents, that are not in your immediate presence. You can recall a high school teacher or a loved one or a favorite pet even if they are not present or if the symbols for those objects are not present. In either case, you can bring them to mind, and their presence or memory causes you to have particular thoughts.

BOX 5.2 Internet Activity: Decoding Meaning

Locate a speech in *Vital Speeches,* using your Infotrac College Edition account. Identify a word in the speech that has contested meanings. That is, find a word that has controversial meanings or meanings that people do not agree upon. Using the semantic triangle, diagram this symbol and its relationship to a thought and object. Which meaning is suggested by the speaker? Did the speaker attempt to persuade the audience to accept a particular meaning for the term? Who is the audience? Do you think the audience agreed or disagreed with the speaker's meaning for the term? How significant was agreement about the meaning of the term to the speech?

The interesting relationship for rhetoricians is that depicted by the bottom dashed line on the triangle in Figure 5.1. According to Ogden and Richards (1928), "there is no relevant relation other than the indirect one" (p. 11). The symbol and the referent, they explained, are not "connected directly" (p. 11). The relationship is only implied or imputed. The word we use for chair could just as easily be the word we use for book. There is nothing natural about calling a book, a book, or a chair, a chair. These relationships are subjective and arbitrary. We agree upon their meanings through social interaction. The Internet Activity for this chapter in Box 5.2 asks you to use the semantic triangle to uncover meaning in a controversial speech.

The following observation may seem fairly obvious to you, but for the readers of Ogden and Richards, it was a profound observation. Ogden and Richards noted that saying a symbol *means* something implies a direct and simple relationship between the symbol and the referent. However, such thinking creates misunderstanding and confusion because the symbol never truly means its referent. In the Critical Insights feature for this chapter (see Box 5.3), we'll consider an example from contemporary culture to explore more fully the relationship between symbols, thoughts, and objects.

The Role of Context in Meaning

Ogden and Richards (1928) identified context as being one of the key reasons why people have different interpretations of symbols. They explained that "the peculiarity of interpretation being that when a context has affected us in the past the recurrence of merely a part of that context will cause us to react in the way in which we reacted before" (p. 53). A sign is a specific kind of stimulus that causes us to react in a particular way to another stimulus we have previously experienced. In other words, if you eat something exotic and don't enjoy the experience, the mere sight of that food in the future or even a symbol for the food will cause you to react negatively to either the object or the symbol. Your future thoughts about that object/symbol have been influenced by your previous experiences with the object. Thus, your interpretation of the symbol or object is shaped by the context in which you previously experienced that object.

BOX 5.3 Critical Insights: The Meaning of School Mascots

The use of Native American nicknames and mascots for high school, college, and professional athletic teams is controversial, to say the least, because of the multiple meanings those symbols may have. The University of North Dakota (UND), for instance, is known as the Fighting Sioux. The word "Sioux" and the Indian head logo used by UND are the symbols involved in this controversy. To those who support the nickname, the symbols cause thoughts of pride—usually in the school's athletic success. Or, for alums, the symbols may cause thoughts of nostalgia for the Alma matter. The object referred to may be a particular UND student athlete or a general image of athletics at the school. For supporters of the nickname and logo, the relationship between the symbols used to support the teams and the teams themselves seems natural and beyond questioning.

However, opponents of the Sioux nickname and logo have different thoughts because of these symbols. For them, the symbols represent the oppression of Native American culture by the white people and the U.S. government. The object, in this case, is generally thought to be a Native American person. Interestingly, the relationship between the symbol and object in this case is more complicated. In fact, the word "Sioux" is a general term, referring to any number of Native American tribes, the Lakota, Nakota, and Dakota. It may be difficult to determine exactly which Native person is being referred to by the word "Sioux." Additionally, the word "Sioux" originated when the French named the native peoples with a word that referred to "enemy" or "snake." Thus, it may not be a flattering symbol to use to refer to a Native person. Of course, the perspective of the symbol user is what determines the kind of implied or imputed relationship between a symbol and an object. The point here is that for supporters of the use of Native American nicknames and logos, the relationships in the semantic triangle seem to be quite stable and natural. For opponents, on the other hand, these relationships are thought to be highly subjective and potentially offensive. As Ogden and Richards (1928) explained, "The fundamental and most prolific fallacy is, in other words, that the base of the triangle given above is filled in" (p. 15).

Let's return to the example of Native American mascots (see Box 5.3). If the context in which you have previously experienced a mascot was purely in an athletic setting, you will have a meaning for the mascot tied to that experience. On the other hand, if the context in which you experienced the word "Sioux" was situated in the struggle between Native and white cultures, then you may have a different meaning for that symbol. The context, here, controls how you ascribe meaning to the symbol.

If you think back to the ancient Greek rhetors and rhetorical theorists, you'll remember that given the oral nature of their culture, they could only speak about events that were present in time and space. That is, they more or less shared in the same context for determining the meaning for words. Thus, their interpretations of symbols were no doubt similar. As time progressed, mediated forms of rhetoric were developed—the printing press in the fifteenth century and radio by the early twentieth century—that changed the contexts in which rhetors and their audiences experienced symbols. People had different contexts for determining meaning, resulting in misunderstanding and, consequently, theories about linguistic reflexivity such as Ogden and Richards'.

Section Thirteen: Postmodernism and Rhetoric

SECTION THIRTEEN: POSTMODERNISM AND RHETORIC

Themes of Postmodernity

Steinar Kvale

Steiner Kvale's survey of postmodern thought shows it going in many directions, its themes not always compatible with one another. Among these themes:

A doubt that any human truth is a simple objective representation of reality.

A focus on the way societies use language to construct their own realities.

A preference for the local and specific over the universal and abstract.

A renewed interest in narrative and story-telling.

Acceptance that different descriptions of reality can't always be measured against one another in any final—i.e., objective and nonhuman—way.

A willingness to accept things as they are on the surface rather than to search (à la Freud or Marx) for Deeper Meanings.

Most of these themes seem to fit together, and yet a certain tension typifies the postmodern condition: on the one hand the tendency toward fragmentation, on the other a search for a larger framework of meaning. Kvale talks about an "expansion of rationality," a belief that reason appears in many guises. This has the makings of another Enlightenment project, a search for the floor plan to a much more spacious Grand Hotel.

It is debatable whether postmodernity is actually a break with modernity, or merely its continuation. Postmodern writers may prefer to write history so that their own ideas appear radically new. Postmodern themes were present in the romanticism of the last century, in Nietzsche's philosophy at the turn of the century, with the surrealists and in literature, for instance in Blixen and Borges. What is new today is the pervasiveness of postmodern themes in culture at large.

"Postmodern" does not designate a systematic theory or a comprehensive philosophy, but rather diverse diagnoses and interpretations of the current culture, a depiction of a multitude of interrelated phenomena.

Postmodern thought is characterized by a loss of belief in an objective world and an incredulity towards meta-narratives of legitimation. With a delegitimation of global systems of thought, there is no foundation to secure a universal and objective *reality.* There is today a growing public acknowledgement that "Reality isn't what is used to be."

In philosophy there is a departure from the belief in one true reality—subjectively copied in our heads by perception or objectively represented in scientific models. There exists no pure, uninterpreted datum; all facts embody theory. In science the notion of an objective reality is an interesting hypothesis, but is not necessary for carrying out scientific work. Knowledge becomes the ability to perform effective actions.

The focus is on the social and linguistic construction of a perspectival reality. In society the development of technology, in particular the electronic media, opens up an increased exposure to a multiplicity of perspectives, undermining any belief in one objective reality. In a world of media, the contrast between reality and fantasy breaks down and is replaced by a hyperreality, a world of self-referential signs. What remains is signs referring to other signs, texts referring to other texts.

A critique of *legitimation* is central in Lyotard's analysis of the postmodern condition. Legitimacy involves the question of what is valid, what is legal, the issue of whether an action is correct and justifiable. Habermas brought the issue to the fore in his book *Legitimation Crisis,* depicting a general loss of faith in tradition and authority, with a resulting relativity of values.

Lyotard identifies "*postmodern* as incredulity towards meta-narratives," as a "paganism," where we pass judgement on truth, beauty and justice without criteria for the judgements. In a comment on the debate between Lyotard and Habermas, Rorty interprets Lyotard as saying that "the trouble with Habermas is not so much that he provides a narrative of emancipation as that he feels the need to legitimize, that he is not content to let the narratives which hold all culture together do their stuff. He is scratching where it does not itch." Rather than continuing the Cartesian attempts of "self-grounding," Rorty advocates a Baconian approach of "self-assertion."

A further theme of modernity is the dichotomy of the *universal and the individual*, between society and the unique person, whereby the rootedness of human activity and language in a given social and historical context is overlooked. In modernity the person is an object for a universal will, or for general laws of history or nature. Or the person is overburdened; man has become the centre of the world, the individual self-feeling being the cornerstone of modern thought, a self stretched out between what it is and what it ought to be.

If we abstract a human from his or her context, we are trapped between the poles of the universal and the individual—the way out is to study humans in their cultural and social context. With the collapse of the universal meta-narratives, the local narratives come into prominence. The particular, heterogeneous and changing language games replace the global horizon of meaning. With a pervasive decentralization, communal interaction and local knowledge become important in their own right. Even such concepts as nation and tradition are becoming rehabilitated in a postmodern age.

The emphasis upon the local surpasses the modern polarity of the universal and the individual, of the objective and the subjective. The local interaction, the communal network, is the point of departure; universal laws and unique individual selves are seen as abstractions from man's being in the world. Rather than equating universal laws with the objective and the individual with the subjective and relative, valid interpretations of meaning and truth are made by people who share decisions and the consequence of their decisions. Instead of a subjective nihilism, we may here talk of a contextual relativism where legitimation of action occurs through linguistic practice and communicative action.

With the collapse of the universal systems of meaning or meta-narratives, a re-narrativization of the culture takes place, emphasizing communication and the impact of a message upon the audience. There is today an interest in *narratives*, on the telling of stories. In contrast to an extrinsic legitimation through appeal to meta-discourses, or Utopia, Lyotard advocates an intrinsic legitimation through a narrative knowledge which "does not give priority to the question of its own legitimation, and . . . certifies itself in the pragmatics of its own transmission without having recourse to argumentation and proof." Narratives themselves contain the criteria of competence and illustrate how they ought to be applied; they are legitimated by the simple fact that they do what they do. A narrative is not merely a transmission of information. In the very act of telling a story the position of the storyteller and the listener, and their place in the social order, is constituted; the story creates and maintains social bonds. The narratives of a community contribute to uphold the values and the social order of that community.

Postmodern thought focuses on *heterogeneous* language games, on the non-commensurable, on the instabilities, the breaks and the conflicts. Rather than regarding a conversation as a dialogue between partners, it is seen as a game, a confrontation between adversaries. A universal consensus of meaning is no ideal; the continual effort after meaning is no longer a big deal. The reply to the modern global sense-makers is simply "just let it be" or "stop making sense."

There exists no standard method for measuring and comparing knowledge within different language games and paradigms; they are incommensurable. A postmodern world is characterized by a continual change of perspectives, with no underlying common frame of reference, but rather a manifold of changing horizons. Rock music videos capture a world of continually changing perspectives and overlapping contexts.

Language and knowledge do not copy reality. Rather, language constitutes reality, each language constructing specific aspects of reality in its own way. The focus is on the linguistic and social construction of reality, on interpretation and negotiation of the meaning of the lived world.

Human language is neither universal nor individual, but each language is rooted in a specific culture, as dialects or as national languages. Current philosophy has undergone a linguistic turn, focusing on language games, speech acts, hermeneutic interpretation, textual and linguistic analysis. The language games take place in local communities; they are heterogeneous and incommensurable. Highly refined expressions in one language, such as poetry, cannot be translated into another language without change of meaning. There exists no universal meta-language, no universal commensurability.

The focus on language implies a decentralization of the subject. The self no longer uses language to express itself; rather the language speaks through the person. The individual self becomes a medium for the culture and its language. The unique self loses prominence; the author is today less an original genius than a gifted craftsman and mediator of the culture through his or her mastery of language.

In postmodern thought there has taken place an *expansion of rationality.* It is not just a "momentary lapse of reason," but a going beyond the cognitive and scientific domain to include also the ethical and aesthetic domains of life in reason. "Modern times" involved a restricted concept of rationality, with a dominance of a technical means-ends rationality. There has been an emphasis on plans and programmes, on calculation, prediction and control. Reason and science have been overburdened with visions of Utopia where all human problems would be solved in the long run by the methods of science and technology.

When the presupposed rationality is seldom found in the given reality, another deeper, more essential reality is constructed to account for the disorder we observe in the world around us. The overstressed conception of a rationality has, in its turn, fostered sceptical reactions in the form of romanticist and irrationalist movements.

Postmodern thought goes beyond a Kantian split of modern culture into science, morality and art, and involves a rehabilitation of the ethical and aesthetic domains. The positivists' split of facts and values is no longer axiomatic; science is a value-constituted and value-constituting enterprise. Appeals to formal logic recede before a rehabilitated rhetoric of persuasion. With the loss of general systems of legitimation, when actions are not justified by appeal to some higher system or idea of progress, the values and the ethical responsibility of the interacting persons become central.

Art is not merely an aesthetic experience, but a way of knowing the world. Rationalist thought has abhorred the non-linear, the imprecise, the unpredictable, and has separated art from science. Mathematicians have been more open to an affinity of science and art, emphasizing the elegance and beauty of models as criteria of truth, cf. for instance *The Beauty of Fractals.*

Postmodern art is characterized by *pastiche* and collage. Art in a postmodern world does not belong to a unitary frame of reference, nor to a project or a Utopia. The plurality of perspectives leads to a fragmentation of experience, the collage becoming a key artistic technique of our time. Styles from different periods and cultures are put together; in postmodern art high-tech may exist side by side with antique columns and romantic ornamentation, the effects being shocking and fascinating. In contrast to modern architecture, tradition is not rejected; nor is it worshipped as in the new classicism. Elements from other epochs are selected and put together in an often ironical recycling of what is usable as decorum. In literature there are collages of texts put together from other texts; the author's individuality and originality are lost in a pervasive use of and references to other texts. Eco's medieval detective novel *The Name of the Rose*, which may be read as a postmodern caricature of the modern meaning hunters, is thus filled with hidden quotes and allusions to other texts.

The reaction against modern rationality and functionalism was visible at an early stage in *architecture*. There was a protest against the functional, against straight lines and square blocks, against the cold logic and boredom of a modern architecture where function preceded form. Postmodern architecture is a reaction against what the painter Hundertwasser has called "the tyranny of the straight line." In the new architecture there is an emphasis on the curvilinear, on the unpredictable, on ornamentation and pastiche and on a non-functional beauty. Reflecting surfaces and labyrinths have become main elements.

On one side there is a return to the medieval village, with its tight-knit community and complex webs of buildings and places. The atriums of the Hyatt Regency Hotels appear as secularized cathedrals with quiet, closed and labyrinthine internal space, with an ornamentation of mixed styles. On the other side there is the Las Vegas trend of architecture, going to the extreme of learning from the most extravagant expressions of current architecture, as expressed in Venturi et al.'s *Learning from Las Vegas.* There is a collage of styles, as in Caesars Palace with its antique statues and parking valets dressed as Roman legionaries. Here there is dominance of the surface, the immense lighted billboards attracting the customer to the less spectacular interior labyrinths of gambling tables and slot machines.

Postmodern thought focuses on the *surface,* with a refined sensibility to what appears, a differentiation of what is perceived. The relation of sign and signified is breaking down; the reference to a reality beyond the sign recedes. In the media, texts and images refer less to an external world beyond the signs than to a chain of signifiers, to other texts and images. A dichotomy of fantasy and reality breaks down or loses interest. There is an intertextuality where texts mainly point to other texts. The TV series *Miami Vice* may refer less to the vice in Miami than to other TV series, imitating and parodying for example the car chases, playing up to the viewer's expectations of a cops-and-robbers series. The image, the appearance, is everything; the appearance has become the essence.

The interest in surface, in what manifestly appears, is in contrast to a debunking attitude where nothing is what it seems to be. This hermeneutics of suspicion, inherent in much modern thought, was carried to its extremes in some versions of psychoanalytic and Marxist thought. An action may never be what it appears to be; rather it is an expression of some deeper, more real reality, a symptom of more basic sexual or economic forces. There is a continual hunt for the underlying plan or rationale, the hidden plot or curriculum, to explain the vicissitudes and disorder of what manifestly appears.

The modern quest for a unitary meaning, where there may be none, has as its pathological extreme the suspicion of paranoia. The debunking attitude may lead to conspiracy theories seeking for the mastermind plot; or, less extreme, to a continual search for an underlying order, constructing a deeper rationality where none is visible.

A postmodern *attitude* involves a suspicion of suspicion, and a refined sensibility to the surface, an openness to the differences and nuances of what appears. It relates to what is given, rather than what has been or what could be—"be cool," "it is no big deal," "no future." The fervent critical attitude of the 1960s and 1970s—as anti-authoritarianism and anti-capitalism—has dissolved. The idea of progress and development, be it the progress of mankind or the individual pilgrim's progress towards salvation of his or her soul, is out. An attitude of tolerant indifference has replaced the involvement and engagement in the social movements and the inner journeys of the 1960s and 1970s. What is left is a liberating nihilism, a living with the here and now, a weariness and a playful irony. Fascination may take the place of reflection; seduction may replace argumentation. There is an oscillation of an intense sensuous fascination by the media and a cool, ironical distance to what appears.

To the existentialists, the discovery of a world without meaning was the point of departure; today a loss of unitary meaning is merely accepted; that is just the way the world is. Postmodern man has stopped waiting for Godot. The absurd is not met with despair; rather it is a living with what is, a making the best of it, a relief from the burden of finding yourself as the goal of life; what remains may be a happy nihilism. With the death of the Utopias, the local and personal responsibility for actions here and now becomes crucial.

Transcending Cultural Usurpation

"What we must learn then is how to conceive difference, without opposition."[1]

It might have been tomorrow, but it surely wasn't yesterday that I found myself in need of the bathroom facilities. I was dressed as a postman, but was really a male man. I stood in an institutionalized hallway. Before me were two doors, for two separate bathrooms. Neither door was labeled with gender specific signification. I capriciously picked one door over the other because at that point indecision was not an option.

Upon entering I could tell by the poly-visual aura and plenty of writing on the wall, that I was in a postmodern water closet. "Postmodernism usually refers to a certain constellation of styles and tones in cultural works: pastiche; a mixture of styles, levels, forms; a relish for copies and repetition; a knowingness that dissolves commitment into irony; acute self-consciousness about the formal, constructed nature of work; pleasure in the play of surfaces; a rejection of history."[2] Postmodernism is pluralistic in regards to the study of society and posits differentiation as a key element in understanding the world. Knowledge is based in the multiplicity of people's perspectives, and rejects the project of universal social science. This rejection links postmodernism to critical theory and poststructuralism in arguing against positivism.

Even knowing these characterizations, I still could not discern if this was the boys bathroom or the girls bathroom. Furthering my way into the room, I absorbed more of the immediate ambience. "The entire elusive phenomenon which has been categorized as postmodernism is best understood not just as a style, but as a general orientation, as what Raymond Williams calls a 'structure of feeling,' as a way of apprehending and experiencing the world and our place, or placelessness, in it."[3] An appropriate atmosphere must be provided for human beings to become self-reflective. The notion of comfort is an essential ingredient for comprehending personal environment. This location, in which I find myself, seems to provide spacious accommodations for a wide variety of opinions. Postmodernism *may* create a conducive climate in which true understanding and appreciation blossoms.

However, my location had no indications of gender. There was no immediate manifestation of a female inclination or sensibility. The lack of this perspective or its seeming absence inherently presented the all too familiar default. The negligence of this facility left me to conclude that I was standing in the men's room. "The absence of discussions of sexual difference in writings about postmodernism, as well as the fact that few women have engaged in the modernism/postmodernism debate, suggests that postmodernism may be another masculine invention engineered to exclude women."[4] This notion seemed to cement the fact that this was a men's room. Nevertheless, voices of female persuasion could be heard. Their origin was yet unclear, but their articulation made sense; " . . . that women's insistence on difference and incommensurability may not only be compatible with, but also may be an instance of postmodern thought."[5]

There I was, thinking I was in one place, then sensing I may be in a different situation. Some wonderfully radical avant-garde modernist had long since adulterized the clear markings on the door and rendered them virtually insignificant. This utilitarianistic vandalism has left me in a compelling haze. This nebulous area impelled me to ponder the essential aspects of difference. "Any discourse which fails to take account of the problem of sexual difference in its own enunciation and address will be, within a patriarchal order, precisely indifferent, a reflection of male domination."[6] The degree of variance between the sexes seems to oscillate between equivocality and truth. One realization that is evident is the existence of representational poverty. Women have unequivocally been misrepresented, misunderstood and at times ostensibly uninvited. This "invitation only" mentality has not escaped the women who have bought advance tickets to shows designed by themselves.

The case of video art serves as an enticing example of women creatively dealing with representation. The 1974 video *Art Herstory,* by Hermine Freed, blatantly, yet with casual elegance, questions the notion of representation; especially within the history of art. Her technical and aesthetic achievements are one in which she superimposes her own live image over masterful artworks of the ages. This certainly addresses the issue of female absence, not so much as subjects but as considerable artists. Looking at these classical paintings with a women superimposed upon them, one is forced to question the female role in contemporary art. This original and lucid representation is an indication of the insightful and powerful images women can create.

Acuminating imagery certainly illustrates the role of woman as subject in Martha Rosler's video, *Vital Statistics of a Model Citizen Simply Obtained,* (1977). Rosler positions herself as the "model" of extreme objectification. Every part of her body is measured and calculated by two male research types. This procedure is coupled with the accompaniment of whistles and bells that signify standard and unacceptable measurements. When the prolonged and odious measurement session is complete the research staff dresses Rosler in traditional women's wear. This explicit example of packaging women as objects is acutely resplendent. The video unquestionably displays the concern of women and their control of representation.

These videos are evidence that women are representing themselves in convincing artistic terms. Craig Owens, who was cited earlier, in discussing women artists in general, proposes a deeper understanding of this representation: "It must be emphasized that these artists are not primarily interested in what representations say about women; rather, they investigate what representation does to women (for example, the way it invariably positions them as objects of the male gaze)."[7] Owens insists that women are and should be part of the discourse concerning postmodernism. Some feminists disagree with what they consider a veiled invitation to a male oriented debate. Martha Gever disagrees with Owens' type of feminism: This type of feminist theory, restricted to the psychic constitution of sexual difference and devoid of materialist or overtly political contextualization, frequently runs aground because of its inability to displace men, white and straight, of course, from their central position."[8]

Patricia Mellencamp furthers this critique of the psuedo-invitation of new-traditionalism. "While many feminists are proudly standing on opposite shores, watching the 'splendid light' of independent films and video tapes and being invited to the intellectual dance of postmodernism by scholars and the art world, we might heed the alarm of the youngest sister, for there are warnings in the academic air of godly wrath and signs of virulent condescension, brazenly heralding a resurgence of reactionary, antifeminist positions."[9] It's quite clear that the debate in question has heretofore begun.

All these voices were echoing and circuiting throughout the empty bathroom that I still stood in pondering my situation. Issues of representation revolve around capacity. The dominion of culture depends primarily on control. Personal control is antecedent to social control. The individual must be regarded before classification. Whereas post feminism may not be an option, meta-feminism may be possible. Meta-critical theory may also be considered a potentiality. The ascension of classification and the wild avoidance of categorization are synonymous with transcendence. Division, the type that causes judgment, is rendered ineffective. Observational skills are not lost, instead they become acutely aware of the beautiful idiosyncrasies of individuals. Spiritual definition overtakes the perpetual stereotyping of groups of people and realizes the specifics of the person.

"The materialist insists on facts, on history, on the force of circumstances; the idealist on the power of thought and will, on inspiration, on miracle, on individual culture."[10] The regularity of self reflection invokes an understanding of the personal. Art often precedes this comprehension which ideally leads to a collective efflorescence of multiple perspectives. Culture is often ruined by cultural debate. "Specialists without spirit, sensualists without heart; this nullity imagines that it has attained a level of civilization never before achieved."[11] Postmodernism, at its best, will not have to invite feminism because it is known all are welcome and political altruism will govern. As illustrated by the earlier mentioned video makers, artists must continually realize and effectuate their identities. "The transcendentalist believes in the perpetual openness of the human mind to a new influx of illumination."[12]

No longer needing the facilities of the bathroom I prepared to depart. Being only a male man and not a postman, I flushed my message down a toilet currently clogged with ill attempts at unity and modernist jargon. However, as a reader of this text you realize that, with the approaching of an androgynous janitor, I had second thoughts.

Notes

1 Craig Owens, "The Discourse of Others: Feminists and Postmodernism," *The Anti-Aesthetic*, Seattle: Bay Press, 1983, p. 62.

2 Todd Gitlin, "Postmodernism: Roots and Politics," *Cultural Politics in Contemporary America*, New York: Routledge Press, 1989, p. 347.

3 Ibid., p. 348.

4 Owens, "The Discourse of Others: Feminists and Postmodernism," p. 61.

5 Ibid., pp. 61–62.

6 Stephen Heath, "Difference," *Screen*, 19, 4, Winter 1978–79, p. 53.

7 Owens, "The Discourse of Others: Feminists and Postmodernism," p. 71.

8 Martha Gever, "The Feminism Factor," *Illuminating Video: An Essential Guide to Video Art*, New York: Aperture Foundation, 1990, p. 229.

9 Patricia Mellencamp, *Indiscretions: Avant-Garde Film, Video and Feminism*, Bloomington: Indiana University Press, 1990, p. 127.

10 Ralph Waldo Emerson's essay, "The Transcendentalist," 1841.

11 Steven Seidman, "Substantive Debates: Perspectives on Modern Culture," *Culture and Society: Contemporary Debates*, Cambridge: Cambridge University Press, 1990, p. 221.

12 Ralph Waldo Emerson's essay, "The Transcendentalist," 1841.